AUTHOR

Péter Mujzer served in the Hungarian Armed Forces for 20 years, graduated from the RCDS (Royal College of Defence Studies, London) and is now a military historian pursuing his PhD with a special interest in the Hungarian Armed Forces during the Second World War. He has already authored fifteen books and over fifty articles on related topics, many of them in English.

PUBLISHING'S NOTES

None of unpublished images or text of our book may be reproduced in any format without the expressed written permission of Luca Cristini Editore (already Soldiershop.com) when not indicate as marked with license creative commons 3.0 or 4.0. Luca Cristini Editore has made every reasonable effort to locate, contact and acknowledge rights holders and to correctly apply terms and conditions to Content.

Every effort has been made to trace the copyright of all the photographs. If there are unintentional omissions, please contact the publisher in writing at: info@soldiershop.com, who will correct all subsequent editions.

Our trademark: Luca Cristini Editore©, and the names of our series & brand: Soldiershop, Witness to war, Museum book, Bookmoon, Soldiers&Weapons, Battlefield, War in colour, Historical Biographies, Darwin's view, Fabula, Altrastoria, Italia Storica Ebook, Witness To History, Soldiers, Weapons & Uniforms, Storia etc. are herein © by Luca Cristini Editore.

LICENSES COMMONS

This book may utilize part of material marked with license creative commons 3.0 or 4.0 (CC BY 4.0), (CC BY-ND 4.0), (CC BY-SA 4.0) or (CC0 1.0). We give appropriate attribution credit and indicate if change were made in the acknowledgments field. Our WTW books series utilize only fonts licensed under the SIL Open Font License or other free use license.

For a complete list of Soldiershop titles please contact Luca Cristini Editore on our website: www.soldiershop.com or www.cristinieditore.com. E-mail: info@soldiershop.com

▲ During the occupation of Transylvania, September 1940, exhauseted Hungarian infantry next to the road, armed with 31 M. carbines. (Fortepan)

Title: **INFANTRY AND ARTILLERY WEAPONS OF THE HUNGARIAN ARMY IN WW2** Code.: **WTW-064 EN**
by Péter Mujzer
ISBN code: 9791255892045 First Edition February 2024
Layout: 177,8x254mm Cover & Art Design: Luca S. Cristini

WITNESS TO WAR (SOLDIERSHOP) is a trademark of Luca Cristini Editore, via Orio, 33/D - 24050 Zanica (BG) ITALY.

WITNESS TO WAR

INFANTRY AND ARTILLERY WEAPONS OF THE HUNGARIAN ARMY IN WW2

PHOTOS & IMAGES FROM WORLD WARTIME ARCHIVES

PÉTER MUJZER

CONTENTS

Introduction .... pag. 5
   Hungarian Armed Forces .... pag. 7
   Defence Industry in Hungary .... pag. 15
Infantry weapons .... pag. 17
   Edged weapons .... pag. 17
   Service pistols .... pag. 19
   Service rifles .... pag. 22
   Machine guns .... pag. 25
   Hand and rifle grenades .... pag. 38
   Land mines .... pag. 42
Infantry heavy weapons .... pag. 43
   Light mortars .... pag. 43
   Mortars .... pag. 43
   Anti tank rifles .... pag. 47
   Handheld rocket-propelled anti-tank weapons .... pag. 49
Anti tank guns .... pag. 53
Artillery .... pag. 65
   Field Artillery .... pag. 65
   Anti-Aircraft Artillery .... pag. 85
   Rocket launchers .... pag. 95
Bibliography .... pag. 97

▲ Hungarian soldier armed with 31 M. carbine, served in Russian in 1942. (Author collection)

INTRODUCTION

Since 1699, Hungary had been part of the Austrian Empire, ruled by the Habsburg dynasty. In 1848/49, the Hungarians staged an uprising seeking their independence, and although the attempt was crushed by the Austrians, it resulted in 1867 that Hungary being granted equal status with Austria. The empire became the dual monarchy of Austria and Hungary. It was known as the kaiserliche und königliche (k. und k.) Monarchy. The kaiserliche part referred to the Imperial throne of Austria, while the königliche part referred to the Royal throne of Hungary. At the end of the First World War, Hungary, as a member of the k. und k. Monarchy ended up on the losing side. Her army disintegrated and her armaments were either taken over or destroyed by the victorious Allied nations. In the autumn of 1919, after the failure of a short-lived Soviet-style republic, a new Hungarian National Army was organised under French supervision. This army was led by a former k. und k. admiral, the highest-ranking native Hungarian military officer, Admiral Miklós Horthy, who was later (in 1920) to become Regent of Hungary, ruling in place of the deposed Habsburgs. Hungary never officially renounced its status as a monarchy, and effectively the nation remained a monarchy without a king until the end of the Second World War.

After WW1, Hungary was in a very critical situation. In 1920 the Allied Powers gave the Hungarian delegation their conditions for peace. This agreement, the Treaty of Trianon, was very similar to the one already imposed on Germany at Versailles, and a French General was later to state that the only result was a twenty-year-long cease-fire, nothing more. The peace conditions for Hungary reduced the area of the country from 282,000 square kilometres to 93,000 square kilometres and the population from 18 million to 9.5 million. Thus 3,263,000 Hungarians became citizens of foreign countries under hostile administrations. The provisions of the Treaty of Trianon reduced Hungary's 1914 industrial base by about 80%.

The Treaty of Trianon was a huge shock for the whole society. The Treaty has left a never-ending scar on the Hungarian national consciousness. Everybody was affected, at least emotional by the harsh conditions of the Treaty. Hungary had lost his imperial status and was reduced to a small country surrounded by hostile states.

The main military aspects of the peace treaty were as follows: Military service based on contracted soldiers, conscription was forbidden, and the army was to consist of no more than 35,000 men. Training of officers was restricted, and the existence of a General Staff was prohibited. The formation of Gendarmerie, Police and Frontier Guard units was also curbed. All war materials, which could be found, were confiscated. The existence or use of guns larger than 105mm calibre, tanks and all heavy armaments was forbidden.

Military aviation and the production of warplanes were prohibited. All warships, except for six small river patrol boats, were forbidden, as was the production and export of guns and gunpowder. Apart from the framework given for the Armed Forces, the production or purchase of arms was generally made impossible. These draconian measures were intended to ensure that the security of the newly created successor states, Romania, Czechoslovakia and Yugoslavia, would be guaranteed, and to maintain the decisive allied military supremacy in the region. It was evident from the very beginning that the nation would not follow these

▲ Hungary's governor, Admiral Miklós Horthy, with his generals during the occupation of Transylvania, in Marosvásárhely, September 16, 1940. Hungary's main objective was to regain the territories lost during World War I. (Fortepan)

dictates if it could be circumvented. Hungarian foreign policy made no secret that it aimed to regain the lost territories. Hungary signed the Treaty of Trianon on 4 June 1920 because it had no other alternative, but her goal was to invalidate the Treaty as soon as possible. Hungarian diplomacy worked to form a close Italian, Austrian and Hungarian relationship in the late 1920s and early 1930s, to avoid isolation and to try to create a better position for Hungary among the European nations. In 1927 Hungary signed a treaty of co-operation with Italy. In the mid-1930s the international political situation changed. Germany had invalidated the Treaty of Versailles and begun to build up a modern regular army. To the Hungarians, Germany seemed to present the opportunity for a good alliance, perhaps providing the only support that Hungary could expect in its quest to recoup her losses of WW1. As previously stated, Hungary's main aim was to regain her lost territories, especially those where Hungarians lived as a majority. However, the military leadership had no illusions about the real potential of the Hungarian Armed Forces. That is why Hungary first focused on a political solution and looked at a military solution as secondary. A comparison of the strengths of the Little Entente's forces with the Hungarian Army reveals the significant differences in size and armaments.

In November of 1938, after the Munich Agreement the Hungarians, due to the Vienna Arbitrage regained Upper-Hungary from Czechoslovakia. The Hungarians occupied Carpathian-Ukraine by force against the Slovakians in March 1939. The next step was the conflict with Romania for Transylvania. The tension between Hungary and Romania reached a peak in summer of 1940, owing to Romania's failure to respond to Hungarian claims to the disputed area of Transylvania. The possibility of a conflict was against the German interest, they intervened, and the second Vienna Arbitrage decided that one part of Transylvania was given back to Hungary. The last step on the road to regaining the lost territory was the participation in the Balkan Campaign against Yugoslavia. In this case, Hungarians gained again former Hungarian territories by force and casualties. Exchange for the German political and military support Hungary had to pay dearly to the Third Reich. In November 1940 Hungary signed an alliance agreement with the Germans which gave extra rights for them. The Germans did not plane to involve directly the Hungarians to the Barbarossa Campaign. Original the Hungarian role was to be a secure communication line, logistic, supply base. But on 26 of June 1941, Soviet fighters strafed a Hungarian train, and three unidentified twin-engine bombers attacked a Hungarian city, Kassa (*Kosice*) not far from the border. These, probably unwilling incidents were enough for the Hungarian Government as "casus belli" to involve into WW1I. It was the output of a strange race between Hungary and Romania for keeping the status quo and for the alliance and goodwill of the Third Reich.

The Hungarians took part in the Eastern Front operations in 1941-44, trying to deploy as few as possible troops to preserving the Hungarian Armed Forces for the end of the war. The Hungarians have become an unreliable ally after Stalingrad and tried to seek the opportunity to left the Axis. It generated the German reaction, the temporary military occupation of Hungary and the replacement of the government by a pro-German one from 19th of March 1944. However, Admiral Horthy remained in position. Most of the population looked at on the Germans rather as brothers in arms than enemies.

A significant Hungarian Jewish population lived in Hungary. Their double-faced status was ended after the German occupation in March 1944. The Hungarian government already proclaimed the so-called "Jewish Acts" in 1938-1944. These legal and administrative rules made their life hard and difficult. Their businesses were taken over by the Hungarian State. The Jews were downgraded to second class citizens. In 1941 the Hungarian government deported 20 000 so-called non-Hungarian citizens from Hungary to Kamenets-Podolsky area. These peoples were executed by the German Einsatzkommandos and their Ukrainian allies. The male, military-aged Jews were called into labour units. Due to the cruel treatment, a lot of Jewish men were killed and lost with the labour units on the Eastern Front. On the other hand, most of them could live better than any other Jewish in occupied Europe until 1944. After the German occupation, their fate was sealed. Most of the Hungarian Jews were deported with willing Hungarian administrative assistance to the German operated concentration camps. During the war, 410-460 000 Hungarian Jews perished, the total casualty of Hungary was 830-950 000 men. In the summer/autumn of 1944, the Red Army arrived on the Hungarian border. The war stepped on the Hungarian soil with its full force and brutality. On 15 of October 1944 Regent Horthy, who had continued his secret negotiations with the Allies, proclaimed an armistice. The armistice was badly organised on the military and political level. The Germans were well informed and well prepared. Horthy was arrested and enforced to hand over his power to Ferenc Szállasi and his Hungarian Nazi "Arrow Cross" movement. The new leader pledged to continue the war until the very end.

HUNGARIAN ARMED FORCES

The Hungarian Army, due to the limitations imposed by the Trianon Treaty, was unable to protect the country. The available manpower was just enough to maintain internal security per the requirements of the Little Entente states Czechoslovakia, Yugoslavia, and Romania. The basic formation of the Army became the mixed brigade, of which seven were organised. The Army also formed four cavalry/hussar regiments and a few support units to arrive at the permitted total of 35.000 men.

The plan was to establish a flexible, powerful and not too expensive basic formation, which later could be used as the cadre for expansion to a larger army. The mixed brigades were composed of two infantry regiments, one-one artillery, bicycle battalions, mortar and cavalry companies plus support units. Seven brigades were organised and were allocated to seven military districts within Hungary. These districts were headquartered at Budapest (1st), Székesfehérvár (2nd), Szombathely (3rd), Pécs (4th), Szeged (5th), Debrecen (6th), and at Miskolc (7th). Following Germany's example, the Hungarian Army began to organise secret units, and to conceal war materials, in direct violation of the dictates of the Trianon Treaty. These extra units were hidden in the branches of the State Police, Customs Service, Gendarmerie and other non-combatant governmental and non-governmental entities such as shipping companies and airlines. The Hungarian Army had a huge number of well-trained officers, both professionals and reservists, who had gained valuable experience with the k. und k. Army in WW1. Many wished to serve, but in an army that was only one-tenth the size of the k. und k. Army, only a small part of them could serve in military units, while the rest were passed to non-military, governmental duties.

The armaments originated from the k. und k. Army, and as such were much worn due to their extensive use during WW1. Forbidden heavy artillery pieces, armoured trains and other prohibited weapons were concealed all around Hungary in civilian stores, cellars or simply dug under the earth to conceal them from the Allied Military Committee. The Hungarian State Railways (MÁV) played a major role in this hid and seek game. Train loads of forbidden materials were transported all around Hungary. Unfortunately, the result of these improper storage conditions was that the majority of the weapons, ammunitions were damaged, rusted and unsuitable for use in case of war.

The output of Hungarian military industries was either confiscated by Romanian forces in 1920 or destroyed by the Allied Military Committee. The greatest prob-

▲ Remains of the past, Rába V.R. truck with 05 M. anti-aircraft gun, painted with WW1 style camouflage, the crew wearing the 17M steel helmet from WW1 too. (Szollár)

▼ Hungarian infantry platoon belonged to one of the Storm Battalion, elite light infantry unit armed with 31 M. light machineguns and 35 M. rifles during the occupation of Upper-Hungary in November 1938. The soldiers wearing the distinctive metal badge, skulk crossed with a hand grenade and dagger on the sleeve of their coats. (Mujzer)

lem of the Hungarian Army was its very poor financial condition, which created a serious obstacle to modernisation and enlargement. Starting in 1927, the pressure from the Allied Committee lessened, and the constant supervision ended.

During the secret rearmament, the Hungarian Army initially concentrated on enlarging the personnel strength and in building up a supply of the equipment forbidden by the Treaty of Trianon. Starting in the mid-thirties, Hungary had a chance to purchase weapons and armaments from Italy and Germany and neutral countries such as Sweden and Switzerland. The home-based military industry was also enlarged following the overall economic situation. By 1938 the Hungarian Army had seven mixed brigades, one cavalry division, (two hussar brigades,) an aviation brigade, an experimental motorised group and the River Forces. Under the direct command of the Chief of the General Staff were two heavy artillery battalions, four anti-aircraft artillery battalions, one signal battalion, one chemical warfare battalion, a motorised transport regiment and an armoured group.

The total strength was 85,000 men, two and half times more than permitted by the peace treaty. 1938 brought a decisive change in the Hungarian Army's situation and development. Relying on the German Italian alliance, and backed by the Polish and Austrian governments, the Hungarian Government revealed its rearmament program.

▲ Hussar squadron entering into a Transylvanian town in September 1940, the troops were welcomed by the native Hungarian population. On the right side of the photo, soldier with armband belongs to the traffic control unit. (MTI)

▼ 39 M. Csaba armoured cars of the Armoured Car Company of the 1st Reconnaissance Battalion and Hussars waiting under the triumph arch in a small Transylvanian village, September 1940. Village people in their dress cloths welcoming the Hungarian troops. (Author's collection)

In March of 5, 1938, Prime Minister Kálmán Darányi announced his government's 1 billion Pengő rearmament program which, disregarding political and financial barriers, was aimed at accelerating the rebuilding of the national defence system within 3-5 years. This rearmament program dealt mainly with the enlargement of the mobile troops and the air force. In the 1936-1937 budget years, the national budget of Hungary was 4.417 million Pengő (almost 1.3 million USD with an exchange rate at that time of 1 USD equalling 3.40 Pengő). This plan provided a boost not only to the army but also to the country, generating many new industries for the military industry. Recognition by the Little Entente states that, from their point of view, the international situation had deteriorated led them to negotiate an equal rearmament pact with Hungary, which was signed in a small Yugoslavian town, Bled on August 22, 1938. As of this time, Hungary's rearmament was legal. However, there remained the problem of the impoverished state of the nation.

After the signature of the Bled equal rearmament treaty, Hungary speeded up the enlarging of its army. The former mixed brigades were expanded to form infantry corps, each with three infantry brigades. The final enlargement plan, called the "Huba Plan", called for the establishment of the following units by 1942:

- 25 infantry brigades, each consisting of two infantry regiments
- 1 cavalry and two armoured divisions
- 2 mountain brigades
- 1 frontier guard brigade
- 1 river forces brigade
- 2 aviation brigades

Due to the restriction of the post-WW1 Peace Treaty of Trianon, the Hungarian Army must base on the contracted soldiers. It lasted until the mid-30s when more and more young men were involved in the military service. From 22 August 1938, the Hungarian Armed Forces switched on the compulsory military service for the male population. From 1940 the Jews were not allowed to serve in combat troops, they drafted into labour companies.

The Hungarian Army inherited, not just the traditions, most of the weapons, equipment, but the military thinking of the K. und K. Armee, which was not surprising taking into the consideration that the military leadership trained, served and fought in the K. und K. Army during WW1. The training and tactical manuals were harmonised and upgraded per the new challenges of the 30s.

The Hungarian mobilisation system based on the duplication of the already existing units, from battalion level up to regiments. In the case of mobilisation, the selected peacetime units halved their strength, their officers and NCOs as well as to give over the activated unit. After that, both units recalled their reservist to fill up the manpower of the units. The existing weapons, equipment, horses, carts, motor vehicles were supplemented from the battalion/regiment and central depots and mobilised civilian horses, carts and vehicles. In theory, it could produce two similar units in a short time. Hungarian units, down to battalion had a cadre unit. In the case of mobilisation, when the active unit was sent to the front the replacement unit remained at home. The replacement unit was responsible for the training of fresh crews and for sending them to the front as replacements. At the end of the war replacement units were organised under each corps into replacement field infantry divisions with reduced staff and armament.

The reservist recalled by mobilisation order delivered by the postmen. Following the mobilisation, the affected units franticly worked on to achieve the readiness in time. A significant part of the supply columns had civilian horses, charts and motor vehicles, which were called in case of mobilisation. The movement control units and the Railway Traffic Coordination Centre worked on to plan, harmonise and execute the railway and road traf-

▲ During the short Yugoslavian Campaign, the Hungarians occupied Voivodina in mid-April 1941, 38 M. Toldi light tank advancing trough the town of Vukovar. (Antoina)

▼ Hungarian troopers belonged to the 15th Bicycle Battalion entering to Kamenyec-Podolsk in July of 1941. Crossing the Carpathian Mountains with the fully kitted 32 M. military bicycle was already an achievement. (War Correspondent Company)

fic to deliver the troops by train as close as possible to the assembly areas.

The manpower strength of the Hungarian Army in case of full mobilisation was 450.000 men in May 1941. Hungarian Army had nine corps organised under three army commands plus the Mobile Corps and the Anti-Aircraft Artillery Corps, one-one aviation and river forces brigades.

In detail, the peacetime organisation and structure of the Hungarian Army consisted of 27 infantry, 4 cavalry regiments, 16 border guards, 9 bicycles, 6 motorised rifles 4 mountain, 2 reconnaissance, 2 armoured cavalries, 2 light tank battalions. The artillery had 97 field, 6 horsed artillery and 28 motorised artillery batteries. Among the motorised artillery were 5 heavy artillery battalions with 13 heavy batteries. The anti-aircraft artillery had 43 batteries, of which 24 were equipped with 80mm guns, the rest had 40 M.m Bofors autocannons.

The Royal Hungarian Air Force had two-two fighter, bomber and one short-range reconnaissance regiments, plus one-one long-range reconnaissance group and paratrooper battalion. The River Forces consisted of 1-1 gunboat and minelayer/river obstacle regiments.

Under the modernisation and mechanisation of the Hungarian Army; the Hungarian military leadership followed the foreign, German, Italian, Soviet military theories concerning the development, organisation and deployment of the mo-

▲ Hungarian troops advancing in the valleys of river Pruth, at Jaremce, due to the demolished bridges in July of 1941 at the Carpathian Mountain, 35 M. FIAT Ansaldo (CV35) tankettes and Ford trucks waiting for passage. (War Correspondent Company)

▼ Curious German Luftwaffe personal gathering around a Hungarian 39 M. Csaba armoured car during the short rest in Ukraine, summer of 1941. The armoured car's turret loopholes and hatches opened for better ventilation. (Antoina)

torised warfare. The first motorised unit of the Hungarian Army, the Experimental Motorised Group, was established in 1932. After the commencement of the re-armament program, the Chief of the General Staff established the Mobile Branch with two cavalry brigades and one motorised brigade, in the spring of 1938.

The 2nd Motorised Brigade was based on the Experimental Motorised Group. It consisted of three motorised rifle battalions, two bicycle battalions, one motorised artillery battalion, one reconnaissance battalion, one-one sapper and signal companies, and one anti-aircraft artillery battery. In October 1938 another motorised brigade, the 1st Motorised Brigade was established with the same strength and organisation as the 2nd Brigade. The Mobile Corps was a complicated and complex unit, consisted of different kind of units; motorised rifle, bicycle, cavalry, reconnaissance, bicycle-tank battalions, supported by motorised, horsed artillery battalions and sapper, signal and supply troops. The Mobile Corps had two-two cavalry and motorised brigades consisted of 6-6 motorised, bicycle, and cavalry battalions. The armoured element consisted of 2-2 reconnaissance, bicycle-tank and armoured cavalry battalions.

In 1942, following the reorganisation of the mobile/armoured troops, one armoured corps was organised with two armoured divisions and one independent cavalry division was set up, however, due to the production delays, the armoured units had no armoured vehicles.

When the 2nd Hungarian Army was mobilised, 9 light infantry division was organised based on the former infantry brigades with improved armament and supporting units. The so-called light infantry divisions consisted of two infantry, one light artillery regiments, signal, engineer battalions, anti-aircraft battery and cavalry squadron as well as supply columns and HQ troops. The 1st Field Armoured Division was set up by ad hoc Hungarian armoured/motorised units supplied by German armoured vehicles, having one-one tank, motorised rifle regiments, two artillery, one-one reconnaissance, anti-aircraft, self-propelled anti-tank/anti-aircraft, engineer, signal battalions and supply, medical, maintenance units. In 1943, following the lessons learned from the current experiences of the operation on the Eastern Front, eight new infantry divisions were organised based on the manpower, armament and equipment of the existing units. Only the 27th "Szekler" Light Infantry Division, dislocated in Transylvania, which kept its original organisation until the end of the war. These new type infantry divisions dislocated in the area of responsibility of each Army Corps. The Corps had one-one new type infantry division and a reserve infantry division.

▲ Hungarian motorised rifles belong to the 1st Motorised rifle Brigade deployed to River Don in summer of 1942. The soldiers armed with 35 M. rifles and 31 M. light machine gun, transported by 38 M. Botond all-terrain squad carrier truck. (Fortepan/Marics)

The 1943 pattern infantry divisions had three infantry and one artillery regiment, one-one reconnaissance, signal, engineer battalions, one-one horsed drawn and motorised supply column. The artillery regiments each four artillery battalions, each with three batteries of four-four 100mm, 105mm and 150mm howitzers. The anti-aircraft battery had twelve 40 M.m 36 M. Bofors autocannons. The infantry regiments were reinforced with 75mm heavy anti-tank gun companies, heavy 120mm mortars and the troops were provided with Hungarian made submachine guns German hand-held anti-tank rockets.

The 1st and 2nd Armoured Divisions had one-one tank and motorised rifle regiments, two-three artillery, one-one reconnaissance, anti-aircraft, self-propelled anti-aircraft, signal, engineer battalions and support, maintenance units, theoretically equipped with Hungarian made armoured vehicles. Due to the combat loses the armoured divisions augmented with German armoured vehicles, weapons too. The 1st Cavalry (later Hussar) Division had three hussar regiment, three-four artillery battalions, one-one reconnaissance, tank, signal, engineer and anti-aircraft battalions and supply units.

The peacetime organisation of the Hungarian Army in 1943 consisted of eight infantry one light infantry divisions, two armoured one cavalry divisions, two mountain brigades, and seven anti-aircraft artillery brigades, River Force Brigade, one Air Force Division and the "Sekler" Border Defence Forces supplemented with troops and units subordinated to the High Command.

The Royal Hungarian Air Force consisted of three aviation brigades and 1st Independent Paratrooper Battalion in 1942-1943. The 1st Aviation Brigade had one-one fighter, bomber long and short-range reconnaissance groups, the 2nd Aviation Brigade had two fighter and one-one bomber and short-range reconnaissance groups, while the 3rd Aviation Brigade was responsible for aviation training with 26 squadrons. The order of battle of 1943-1944 consisted of one Aviation Division with two combat and one training brigades. The brigades had one long and two short-range reconnaissance groups, two bomber and three fighter groups with 392 combat aircraft. The Aviation Training Brigade had 432 planes. The paratrooper battalion was enlarged to the 1st Paratrooper Regiment with two paratrooper battalions and regimental support troops.

▲ Heavy weapons of the 1st Motorised Rifle Regiment put on display in 1944, consisted of 40 M. Nimród self-propelled anti-aircraft canons, 75mm Pak 40 anti-tank gun, light and medium machine guns on anti-aircraft tripods. The officers wearing cavalry spurs. (Szollár)

▼ Heavily camouflaged Hungarian Skoda 38(t) tank hiding alongside a mud hut in a Ukrainian village in summer of 1942, during the bridgehead battles. The tanks painted in German panzer grey wearing the Hungarian octagonal military insignia. (Author's collection)

▲ During the fighting at Galicia in April 1944, the Hungarians deployed their home-developed assault artillery pieces, the 40/43 M. Zrínyi assault howitzers served with the 1st Assault Artillery Battalion, the white 3 painted on the back of the vehicle stand for the 3rd Battery. (Szollár)

▼ Soviet officers evaluate a captured Hungarian 40 M. Turán medium tank at Galicia in July of 1944. The Hungarian tank belonged to the 3rd Tank Regiment, 2nd Armoured Division, that time the 40 M. Turán tank was outdated to fight against the Soviet T-34 tanks. (Russianphoto.ru)

▲ The Hungarian Occupation forces due to the different size gauge operated captured ex-Soviet armoured trains to control and protect the railway lines in Ukraine and Belarussia. The armoured trains were armed with mixed ex-Soviet and Hungarian armaments. (Fortepan/Kókány)

▲ In September 1944, the 2nd Hungarian Army tried to fight back South-Transylvania, the troops were supplemented by 75mm Pak 40 heavy anti-tank guns confiscated from weapon transports addressed to the Romanians before changing side. The guns towed by RSO tracked light artillery tractor.(Szollár)

▲ The pride of the Hungarian Army, the 1st Cavalry Division was deployed to Belarussia in summer of 1944, its 15th Bicycle Battalion had a self-propelled anti-aircraft platoon armed with two 40 M. Nimród vehicle. The divisional sign painted in white on the front plate of the Nimród. (Szollár)

▼ Hungarian soldiers in full combat order, armed with 35 M. rifles, the soldier, third from left armed with Hungarian made 9mm 39 M. Király submachine gun in summer of 1944. (Author's collection)

▲ After the siege of Budapest abandoned German hand-held anti-tank weapons, ammunition and grenades left behind in an abandoned firing position in early 1945. (Fortepan 60130)

▼ The 1st Hungarian Army was reinforced with the Hungarian 7th Assault Artillery Battalion, equipped with StuG. III assault guns deployed around Makó. The command vehicle of 1st Lieutenant Kőszeghy knocked out by Soviet tanks in close-quarter combat in 26 September. (Bonhardt)

▲ Captured Hungarian officers guarded by a Soviet soldier armed with PPS sub-machine gun. Among the Hungarian prisoners are Air Force and Army officers, on the left one of them wearing a typical cavalry jacket. (Fortepan/Vörös Hadsereg)

▼ Workshop of the Hungarian Automobile Depot at Mátyásföld in 1943, the factory level maintenance and repair of the Hungarian armoured and soft-skin vehicles were carried out there. (Fortepan/Lissák).

DEFENCE INDUSTRY IN HUNGARY

Following the end of World War I, the Hungarian military industry was in bad shape. The lost resources of her territories ceded to other nations, manpower losses caused by the war, and the limitations imposed by the Treaty of Trianon all played their part in this situation. During the late 1920s and early 1930s, the economic situation of the country began to improve. Hungary's economy was essentially based on agriculture, and those industries which existed did so mainly to provide tools and equipment meant for use in agriculture. However, a small number of famous heavy industrial companies which originated in the old k. und k. period played a very important role in the military industry. The Hungarian heavy industry producing war materials also came from the old Austro-Hungarian period, trying to survive the post-war decline and restrictions. In 1922, a State Arsenal was organised to conceal the possible developments and production of the Hungarian military industry. From the 1930s, the Manfred Weiss, FÉG, Diósgyőri State Ordnance Factory, Ganz, MÁVAG, Magyar Vagon és Gépgyár (Rába), GAMMA, and Danuvia companies provided the backbone to the Hungarian military industry. The factories closely cooperated with the Military Technology Institute of the Hungarian Army (HTI), which was responsible for research and standardisation of armament and equipment. Due to financial constraints, these companies initially focused on repairs and modifications to existing equipment, but later worked on production under license and independent developments.

The Weiss Manfred Factory as the flagship of the war industry was responsible for manufacturing ammunition, aircraft, automobiles and armoured vehicles.

The FÉG Factory (Weapon and Machinery Factory) already produced infantry weapons during WW1, the Factory continued to produce rifles, pistols and started to manufacture the Schwarzlose machine guns. Danuvia Factory produced light machine gun under licence and home designed submachine guns. The Diósgyőri State Ordnance Factory was responsible for repairing, modifying the old WW1 artillery pieces and producing new models mostly under Swedish Bofors licences.

The GAMMA, MOM, Tungsram and Telephone Factories provided the mechanical and elector engineering products for the Army, such us field radios, telephones, binoculars, optics for artillery and infantry weapons, range finders, fire control and direction devices.

The Magyar Vagon és Gépgyár (RÁBA) and MÁVAG Factories produced trucks, the Hoffherr Factory made artillery tractors and Uhri Company built the Hungarian superstructure for the Krupp and Hansa Lloyd vehicles.

▲ Assembly line of the GANZ Factory at Budapest in 1942, the hull of the 40 M. Turán medium tank prepared for assembly. (Bonhardt)

As the basis of the weaponry of the Hungarian Armed Forces given by the Peace Treaty in quantity type by type as follows:
- Infantry rifles, carbines 57776, remanufacturing by the wear and tear
- Service pistols 28822, remanufacturing by the wear and tear
- Machine guns 560, remanufactured by the wear and tear
- Submachine guns 600, although allowed, was not in service
- Light artillery pieces 129, remanufacturing by the wear and tear
- Mortars 70, remanufacturing by the wear and tear
- Ammunition for rifles 33521850 cartridges, 11662611 could be produced yearly
- Ammunition for service pistols 7484850 cartridges, 1727650 could be produced yearly
- Artillery shells 124000, 12400 could be produced yearly
- Mortar shells 52500, 3500 could be produced yearly
- Hand grenades 350000, 175000 could be produced yearly
- Cavalry sabres 21461, remanufacturing by the wear and tear

These weapons inherited from the K. und K. Armee used by the Hungarian troops during the Great War and after that during the short-lived communist regime, defending the country borders from the invading Czech, Romanian and Serbian Armies in 1919.

By the end of the WW2, the Hungarian Defence Industry was able to supply the Army and the Air Force with the full spectrum of weaponry. The Army was supplied with Hungarian made armoured vehicles, artillery, infantry weapons and trucks, the River Forces equipped with Hungarian designed and made armoured and minelayer-sweeper boats, the Air Force got the Hungarian made Me 109G and Me 210 planes too.

▲ Spare parts storage of the Hungarian Automobile Depot at Mátyásföld, transmission gear of a Turán tank inspected by the crew, behind them are spare pistons in 1943. (Fortepan/Lissák)

INFANTRY WEAPONS

EDGED WEAPONS OF THE HUNGARIAN ARMY WW2

The edged or bladed weapon is a melee weapon with a cutting edge. Bladed weapons include swords, daggers, knives, and bayonets. Armies of WW2 primarily relied on firearms for combat, but melee weapons still played a role in specific situations. Some of the most common edged weapons used by the troops during WW2 include bayonets, trench knifes/ storm knife and cavalry swords. The Hungarian Army used ceremonial, dress and combat edged weapons inherited from the WW1 Austro-Hungarian Army as well as home designed ones.

Bayonets
Bayonet is a knife, dagger, sword, or spike-shaped melee weapon designed to be mounted on the end of the barrel of a rifle, carbine, allowing the gun to be used as an improvised spear in close combats. The Hungarian Army used different service rifles from 1920 until 1945, all they had their own bayonets.

95 M. bayonet
There were two main variants of the bayonet; the first was the standard bayonet, the second was the NCO variant that featured a hooked quillion and a golden lanyard. The overall length was 360 millimetres (14 in) and the blade was 248 millimetres (9.8 in) long. The bayonet was unusual in that the edge faced upwards when mounted on the rifle. The 31 M. and 31/a M. rifles used the same bayonets as the 95 M. rifles.

35 M. bayonet
Straight, symmetrical bladed knife bayonet in a tin sheath painted in olive-green. The blade is sharpened on both sides and is reinforced by a rib at the front and back, which protrudes sharply at the blade tip and then gradually flattens towards the point. The method of attaching the bayonet is almost identical to the one used on the French Lebel rifle bayonet. The bayonet was made with a surprisingly long blade, which was impractical because when it was fixed to the rifle it was difficult to move with it. Carried the bayonet in scabbard, attached to the belt was also impractical, because it was easy to get caught up in everything. The 35 M. bayonets also used for the 43 M. rifles, the 39 M., 39/a M. and 43 M. submachine guns.

Technical characteristics

Specification	95 M. bayonet	31 M. bayonet	35 M. bayonet
Country of origin	Austro-Hungary	Austro-Hungary	Hungary
Manufacturer	Steyer, FÉG	Steyer, FÉG	FÉG
Overall Length	360 mm	360 mm	495 mm
Length of the blade	248 mm	248 mm	340 mm

17 M. trench/storm knife
The normal bayonets were too long for trench fighting, the trench or storm knife was invented by the troops at the frontlines. It was a knife with a conical, tapered, spear-shaped blade. The blade has a short false edge at the top and four notches on the back of the blade near the guard. The knife has a small ellipsoidal cross guard with the upper quillion bending towards the handle and a smooth, round wooden handle fixed with three rivets. Simple, smooth metal sheath. A metal plate is riveted to one side, from which two metal loops protrude, through which a leather loop is sewn, acting as a belt loop. After the WW1, it disappeared from the weaponry. By the mid-30s, in accordance with the establishment of the light infantry units; grenadier companies and jager battalions it came back to the service. The trench/storm knife, in some documents called as hunting knife were issued to light infantry troops, later to the paratroopers, mountain reconnaissance and storm troopers of the Hungarian Army.

04 M. cavalry sword
The sword originated from the Austro-Hungarian Army, it had an enlisted and officer version, which differed only sword handles, the officer one was more sophisticated. Mounted; cavalry, horsed artillery officers could wear it, in dismounted mode too, in normal everyday activity as well as for dress and parade occasions. How-

▲ 31 M. rifles with fixed 95 M. bayonets in scabbards ready for weapon inspection at a railway construction unit in 1938. (Fortepan/Lissák)

◄ The Austro-Hungarian origin and modified rifles, carbines had the 95 M. knife bayonet. On this stage photo the soldier had the 35 M. steel helmet, 31 M. carbine with 95 M. bayonet. (Fortepan/Konok)

▲ Hungarian motorised rifles riding on their 38 M. Botond squad carrier armed with the 8mm 35 M. rifle and 35 M. spike bayonet. The bayonet was too long, unpractical but it looked awesome. (War Correspondent Company)

ever, as combat edged weapon it belonged to the cavalry/hussar officers, NCOs and enlisted men as well as. The scabbard was attached to the saddle and was carried in operations until the end of 1941. From 1942 it was removed from the combat equipment and was saved for parades. It was quiet a popular item among the officers and frequently non-mounted officers worn the sword risking penalty of non-issued equipment.

61 M. infantry dress sword
It also originated from the Austro-Hungarian Army, by the time it just had ceremonial role worn by non-mounted officers. As it was more fragile looking sword it was less popular among the officers.

Technical characteristics

Specification	17 M. trench /storm knife	04 M. cavalry sword	61 M. infantry dress sword
Country of origin	Austro-Hungary	Austro-Hungary	Austro-Hungary
Manufacturer			
Overall length	373 mm	1027 mm	911-1011mm
Length of the blade	324 mm	860 mm	750-850 mm
Weight of the weapon		1070 gr	800 gr
Weight of the scabbard		860 gr	510 gr

SERVICE PISTOLS

After the WW1 the Hungarian Army operated the service pistols and revolvers of the Austro-Hungarian Army. They wanted standardised the service pistols with low cost, chosen an already existing type.

19 M. Frommer Stop 7,65mm service pistol
The pistol was a long recoil operated automatic pistol designed by Rudolf Frommer, Georg Roth and Karel Krnka. The pistol was adopted by the Hungarian reserve element of the Austro-Hungarian Army, the Honvédség, chambered for 7,65mm. In 1919 it was accepted by the Royal Hungarian Army as 19 M. service pistol, and it was produced by 1930. A 9mm version, 39 M. was designed, but did not go into production. It was well-made from excellent materials, somewhat ugly, but not as awkward as it looks, and it had a good reputation. However, by the late 20s its 7,65mm calibre was not meet the standards of military service pistol. It was more a staff officer's weapon than first line combat weapon.

29 M. and 37 M. 9mm service pistol
In the late 20s, the Army decided to replace the mixed WW1 and Frommer Stop pistols with a simpler and unified had weapon. Frommer offered his 9mm pistol, a simple and robust blow-back weapon, serviceable and reliable and went into service as the 29 M. service pistol produced by FÉG Factory. Due to the expansive interest of the Army, a modified pistol the 37 M. was developed and accepted by the Hungarian Army. It was an upgrade of the previous one produced in large quantity for German export too. The German version made with 7,65mm calibre. From 1938 to 1944 the FÉG produced 245103 37 M. service pistols

Technical characteristics

Country of origin	Hungary	Hungary	Hungary
Specification	19 M. service pistol	29 M. service pistol	37 M. service pistol
Manufacturer	FÉG	FÉG	FÉG
Calibre	7,65mm	9mm	9mm
Weight	600g	730g	730g
Length	165mm	170mm	170mm
Barrell length	96mm	100mm	100mm
Magazine	7 rounds	7 rounds	7 rounds
Muzzle velocity	320 m/s	263 m/s	263 m/s
Rate of fire	20 rounds/minute	20 rounds/minute	20 rounds/minute
Range	50-100 meters	50-100 meters	50-100 meters

▲ The 04 M. cavalry sword was attached to the saddle of the cavalry, which did not obstruct the hussars, when they dismounted for combat. (Mujzer)

▼ The cavalry also used the 04 M. cavalry swords for ceremonial occasions, here an assault artillery training unit junior NCO salute with his sword, the rest armed 35 M. rifles. (Mujzer)

▲ Young reserve Ensign belonged to the mobile troops in dress uniform and 61 M. infantry sword. (Original colour photo)

▲ Paratroopers folding and packing their parachutes, the soldier the right issued with the quiet simply designed WW1, 17 M. trench knife. (Fortepan/Horváth)

▲ Lt. Collonel Zoltán Pisky commander of the 1ˢᵗ Mountain Battalion in 1941, saluting with his 61 M. infantry sword. At right: a Frommer Fémáru Model Pistole 37 M. below: a Young reserve officer candidate posing with his 7,65mm 19 M. pistol. The Frommer Stop pistol did not meet the standards of the 30s but retained and used in large quantity by the Army. (Fortepan/Dienes)

▲ Firing practice of the officer candidates with 9mm 37 M. pistols, they wear the ammunition pouches, 35 M. bayonet and steel helmet. (Fortepan/Ludovika)

SERVICE RIFLES

During the WW2 the fire power of the Hungarian infantry still rested on the bolt action rifles. The first line infantry was equipped with the home invented and produced 35 M. rifles, however the reserve infantry, combat support troops had 95 M., 31 M. service rifles. The Hungarians used a significant number of captured 7,92mm Mauser rifles of Czech, Polish and Yugoslavian origin. Due to the lost September War in 1939, the rearmed Polish troops handed over 20500 7,92mm Mauser, 8500 French rifles. In 1939 4700 Czech Mauser and Manlicher rifles were captured from the Slovakian Army and 13000 different rifles the Yugoslavian Army in 1941.

95 M. 8 mm service rifle

The Mannlicher M1895 was an Austro-Hungarian straight pull bolt-action rifle, designed by Ferdinand Ritter von Mannlicher that used a refined version of his revolutionary straight-pull action bolt Mannlicher M1890 carbine. The primary manufacturers were the ŒWG in Steyr, and FÉG in Budapest. Originally they were chambered for the round nosed 8×50mmR cartridge, but almost all of the rifles were rechambered to accept the more powerful 8×56mmR cartridge in the 1930s. When the independent Hungarian state emerged after the WW1, the 95 M. rifles and its variants were the main bolt action rifles of the Hungarian Army as well as the Gendarme and the Police. However, in early 30s the it was redesigned for the new, modern ammunition.

Technical characteristics

Country of origin	Austro-Hungary	Austro-Hungary
Specification	95 M. service rifle	95 M. service carbine
Manufacturer	Steyr/FÉG	Steyr/FÉG
Calibre	8mm 8x50mmR	8mm 8x50mmR
Weight	3,80 kg	3,4 kg
Length	1272 mm	990 mm
Barrel length	765 mm	500 mm
Magazine	5 rounds integral box, clip loaded	5 rounds integral box, clip loaded
Muzzle velocity	620 m/s	620 m/s
Range	1950 meters	1950 meters
Rate of fire	10-15 rounds/minute	10-15 rounds/minute
Bayonet	95. M knife bayonet	95 M. knife bayonet

31 M. 8mm service rifle

The Hungarian Army retained the 95 M. straight-pull 8mm Mannlicher rifle until adopted a new cartridge in 1931, named Mannlicher 31 M. rifle. The original 95 M. rifles were re-barrelled in great quantities to take the new cartridge. However, the new cartridge caused problems at extractions due to the higher chamber pressure. After the First World War, most long rifles had to be cut to carbine length under the peace treaty. In 1930, the Austrians replaced the old 8x50R ogival ammunition with the more modern, flatter trajectory, higher-portion 8×56R pointed ammunition. The Hungarian Army followed the Austrian example and in 1931 introduced the 8X56R ammunition under the name of 31 M. rifle cartridge. The 31 M. rifles were intended to be kept in service until the arrival of the new rifle planned to replace them. The 31/a M. version was the converted 95 M. long-barrel rifle. After 1938, Hungarian soldiers in rifle companies were reequipped with the new 35 M. rifle, but the most of troopers (machine gunners, supply troops, pioneers, gunners, messengers etc.) were still equipped with Mannlichers. In mid-1940 the Hungarians had 565.000 rifles. Of this, 105.000 were new 35 M. and the rest were Mannlicher, by variants:

- 100.000 95 M. (7.62 chambered, purchased from Germany, used in second-line units)
- 11.000 89/90 M. (given from Austria in return for debts)
- 349.000 31 M. (old rifles converted to 8x56 standard and post-war FÉG production)

▲ Admiral Horthy reviewing the troops armed with 95 M. Manlicher rifles, wearing old Austro-Hungarian uniform and 17 M. steel helmet. (Author's collection)

▼ Staged photo of a Hungarian soldier armed with 31 M. carbine with fixed 95 M. bayonet aiming in the old fort of Kamenyec-Podolski, Ukraine, summer of 1941. (War Correspondent Company)

▲ Dispatch rider belonged to the 1st War Correspondent Company, riding on a Zündapp DB motorbike, wearing leather protective suit and Italian style crash helmet, armed with 31 M. carbine, at the River Don, 1942. (Fortepan/Konok)

▲ Reserve officer cadets in light weighted summer uniform, armed with the 8mm 31 M. carbines, and just one double ammunition pouch. (Fortepan)

Technical characteristics

Country of origin	Hungary	Hungary
Specification	31 M. service rifle	31/a M. service carbine
Manufacturer	FÉG	FÉG
Calibre	8mm 8X56R	8mm 8X56R
Weight	3,3 kg	3,3 kg
Length	1005 mm	1005 mm
Barrel length	498 mm	518 mm
Magazine	5 rounds integral box, clip loaded	5 rounds integral box, clip loaded
Muzzle velocity	680 m/s	680-720 m/s
Range	2000 meters	2000 meters
Rate of fire	10-15 rounds/minute	10-15 rounds/minute
Bayonet	95 M. knife bayonet	95 M. knife bayonet

35 M. 8mm service rifle
The 35 M. repeating rifle is a Hungarian-developed rotary bolt action rifle, produced by FÉG until the end of World War II. Basically, a new design, it bears some resemblance to the 31 M. repeating rifle (carbine). It was put into service in 1936. This was the last Mannlicher to be adopted as service weapon, redesigned to fire their improved 31 M. rimmed cartridge the 8×56 mm R. The rifle was shortened to more handy proportions. The result was a serviceable rifle using the protruding Mannlicher clip-loaded magazine, a two-piece stock and bolt handle, which locked down ahead of the receiver bridge. The first line infantry/rifle companies were armed with the 35 M. By the time of the invention and design of the 35 M. bolt action rifle, the direction of development were the automatic rifles.

Technical characteristics

Country of origin	Hungary
Specification	35 M. service rifle
Manufacturer	FÉG
Calibre	8mm 8X56 R
Weight	4,04 kg
Length	1106 mm
Barrell length	600 mm
Magazine	5 rounds integral box, clip loaded
Muzzle velocity	730 m/s
Range	2000 meters
Rate of fire	20 rounds/minute
Bayonet	35 M. spike bayonet

43 M. 7,92mm service rifle
The 43 M. repeating rifle is a Hungarian German developed rotary bolt action repeating rifle, which fires the German 7,92×57 mm Mauser cartridge. It has been developed to meet the Axis' need for ammunition uniformity, using and modifying the Hungarian 35 M. repeating rifle. The modifications affected the barrel (complete barrel replacement), the piston button grip was curved downwards, the ability to mount German Mauser bayonets was modified, the barrel strap was changed (the strap was moved transversely on the receiver, following the Mauser pattern), and the Mauser magazine was fitted with a more closed and double-row Mauser magazine frame (the lower bedding was also modified for this reason). Although the Mauser lock was replaced by the Mannlicher lock, which has been used in Hungary for a long time, it still shows several

similarities with the Karabiner 98K as described. The FÉG produced the type from mid-1941 until the end of World War II to German orders, and the Third Reich commissioned it as Gewehr 98/40 (or Infanterie Gewehr 98/40), with the first delivery on 13 October 1941. According to the ammunition standardisation the Germans convinced the Hungarians for the conversion and in 1943 Hungarian Army put it into service as the 43 M. repeating rifle. The two types differ slightly from each other. Altogether 230.000 rifles were produced, 138.400 for the Germans and 90.000 for the Hungarians.

Technical characteristics

Country of origin	Hungary
Specification	43 M. service rifle
Manufacturer	FÉG
Calibre	7.92mm 7.92x57
Weight	4,1 kg
Length	1110 mm
Barrell length	600 mm
Magazine	5 rounds integral box, clip loaded
Muzzle velocity	755 m/s
Range	2000 meters
Rate of fire	20 rounds/minute
Bayonet	35 M. spike or 98 M. knife bayonet

▲ Rifle 8mm 31 M. Mannlicher carbine, below: the rifle 8mm 35 M.. At right: 95 M. bayonet and his scabbard.

SUBMACHINE GUNS

At the beginning of the Hungarian top brass was not enthusiastic about the submachine guns, saw it as rather an internal security weapon than a military one at first. However, the combat operations on the Eastern Front made it obvious that the submachine guns were dearly needed to improve the firepower of the Hungarian infantry. In contrast with the Hungarians the Red Army was amply supplied with submachine guns, self-loading rifles and machine guns.

35/I M. 9mm Bergmann submachine gun

The prototype was made in 1932, in Denmark, due to the peace treaty restrictions. The first 2000 MP34 went to the German police and was exported to Bolivia. It had a right-hand side-feeding magazine. It fired semi-automatic, when the trigger was pulled half-way and full automatic, when it was pulled further back. In 1935 some modifications were applied, simplifying the production and improve the reliability. According to photo evidence as early as 1938-1939 Hungarian clandestine sabotage unit, Ragged Guard was armed with

▲ Hungarian troops stand attention, wearing greatcoat, 35 M steel helmet with decorative oak leaf attached to the ventilation hole, armed with 8mm 35. M rifles with fixed bayonets. (Author's collection)

▼ The 9mm 35/I M. Bergmann submachine guns were issued to the clandestine, paratrooper and storm trooper units to improve the fire power. Storm troopers practising bunker demolition during the summer of 1940. (Mujzer)

▲ Paratrooper posing with a 9mm 35/I M. Bergmann submachine gun, double ammunition pouch and 37 M. holster, wearing the paratrooper overall and 35 M. steel helmet. (Author's collection)

▲ Bicycle troops armed with 8mm 35 M. rifles, attached to the frame of their bicycles, behind them is a 38 M. Botond squad carrier truck with motorised rifles in April of 1941. (Fortepan)

MP35, naming by the Hungarian 35 M. submachine guns. In 1940 the paratroopers and the assault engineers were equipped with German 35 M. Bergman 9mm submachine guns. The 1st Paratrooper Battalion got 1000 35 M. Bergman submachine guns in 1940.

Technical characteristics

Country of origin	Germany
Specification	35/I M. 9mm submachine gun
Manufacturer	Bergmann
Calibre	9mm Parabellum
Weight	4,30 kg
Length	840 M.m
Barrel length	180 mm
Magazine	22 or 32 rounds
Muzzle velocity	350 m/s
Range	200 meters
Rate of fire	350 rounds/minute

39 M. 9mm Király submachine gun

The submachine gun was designed by Hungarian weapon's engineer Pál Király in the late 1930s, and was produced by the Danuvia Company. The guns were issued to the troops in 1939 and remained in service throughout World War II. The 39 M. was a large, sturdy weapon, like a carbine. Inspired by the SIG MKMS, the submachine gun used the more powerful 9×25mm Mauser round, and incorporated lever-delayed blowback in order to better manage this high energy cartridge. The magazine can be folded forward into a recess in the stock where a plate then slides over it. The gun was well-liked by troops; it functioned well in the sub-zero, muddy conditions on the Eastern Front. The only difficulty was the availability of 9×25mm Mauser ammunition. The Király submachine guns had 35 M. bayonet. 1566 were ordered from the Danuvia Factory in 1940, but the submachine guns did not arrive at the troops until 1943. The 39 M. submachine gun was too long not suited for paratroopers, a folding wooden stock version; 39/a M. was manufactured in limited numbers to reduce the weapon's length during the combat jump.

Technical characteristics

Country of origin	Hungary	Hungary
Specification	39 M. 9mm submachine gun	39/a M. 9mm submachine gun
Manufacturer	Danuvia	Danuvia
Calibre	9mm Mauser	9mm Mauser
Weight	4,15 kg	4,24 kg
Length	1048mm	1048mm/784mm with folded butt
Barrell length	500 mm	500 mm
Magazine	40 rounds	40 rounds
Muzzle velocity	450 m/s	450 m/s
Range	650 meters	650 meters
Rate of fire	650-780 rounds/minute	760-780 rounds/minute

43 M. 9mm Király submachine gun

Later a new 43 M. submachine gun was developed with pistol grip and steel folding-but; it also fired 9mm Mauser cartridges from the 40-round box magazine. This gun works like the 39 M., but most of its parts have been modified. The stock can be folded under the frame, it has two metal rods covered with wood and receives a folding butt plate. The magazine can also be folded under the frame, but its design differs from that of the 39 M. The 43 M. magazine is not the same as that used for the 39 M. Between 5,000 and 9,000 43 M. submachine guns were produced in 1944. A 44 M. variant, without a shoulder stock, was also made but was not adopted.

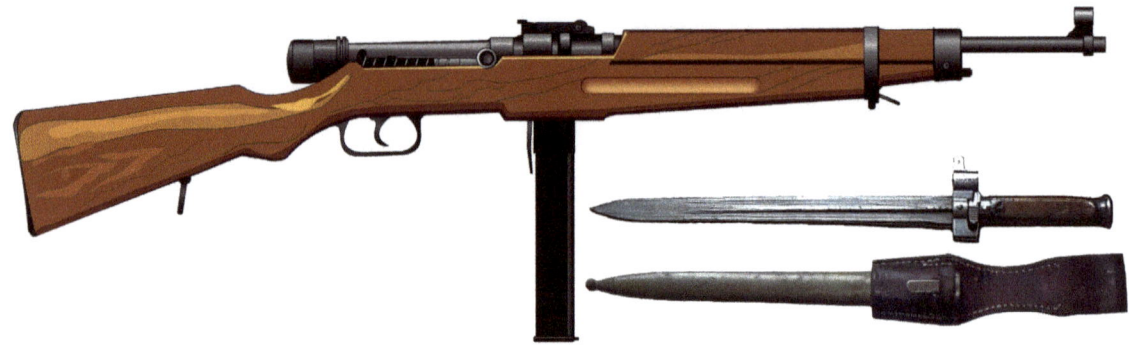

▲ 39 M. 9mm Király submachine gun. This submachine gun was issued with a standard 35 M. type Sword bayonet

▲ 43 M. 9mm Király submachine gun.

Technical characteristics

Country of origin	Hungary
Specification	43 M. 9mm submachine gun
Manufacturer	Danuvia
Calibre	9mm Mauser
Weight	3,7 kg
Length	950mm/750mm with folded stock
Barrell length	425 mm
Magazine	40 rounds
Muzzle velocity	450 m/s
Range	600 meters
Rate of fire	650-700 rounds/minute

40 M. Schmeisser 9mm submachine gun

Designed in 1938 by Heinrich Vollmer with inspiration from its predecessor the MP 38, it was heavily used by squad and platoon commander. The MP 40 submachine guns are open-bolt, blowback-operated automatic weapons. The only mode of fire is automatic, but the relatively low rate of fire permits single shots with controlled trigger pulls. Although the MP 40 was generally reliable, a major weakness was its 32-round magazine. The MP 40 uses a double-column, single-feed version. The single feed inserts resulted feed failures; this problem was exacerbated by the presence of dirt or other debris. The troops of the 2nd Hungarian Army got 5000 German MP 40 submachine guns named as 40 M. submachine gun in 1942, to arm the squad, platoon and company commanders at the infantry. The ammunition resupply depended on the German logistic chain which sometimes caused delays.

▲ The first Hungarian designed and produced submachine gun was the 9mm 39 M. Király submachine gun, it was intentionally as lengthy as a rifle. Firing the powerful Mauser cartridges. At right: Mountain troop's reserve officer candidate firing with the 9mm 39 M. Király submachine gun. The submachine gun had the Hungarian designed ammunition holster containing six magazines, 240 cartridges, plus one magazine was in the weapon. (Author's collection) Below: The captured Soviet 7,62mm PPS submachine guns were prized weapons of the Hungarians, easy to handle, maintain, plenty of ammunition. (Mujzer)

▲ Seasoned trooper of the 51st Self-propelled Armoured Autocannon Battalion armed with 9mm 40 M. submachine gun, in the spring of 1943, Ukraine. (Fortepan/Miklós) In the small photo: the shortened version of the 39 M. was the 43 M. submachine gun with foldable stock, normally used by the platoon and company commander at the end of the war. (Illésfalvi)

Technical characteristics

Country of origin	Germany
Specification	40 M. 9mm submachine gun
Manufacturer	Erfurter Maschinenfabrik
Calibre	9mm Parabellum
Weight	4,2 kg
Length	625mm, 856mm with extended butt
Barrell length	230mm
Magazine	32 rounds
Muzzle velocity	365 m/s
Range	200 meters
Rate of fire	500 rounds/minute

LIGHT MACHINE GUNS

The light machine gun is a light-weight machine gun designed to be operated by a single infantryman on bipod, with or without an assistant, as an infantry support weapon. Based on the experiences of the WW1, the Hungarians also adopted the light machine guns to support the infantry, cavalry troops in combat. The first light machine gun was purchased from Denmark, the standard squad light machine gun was the 31 M. 8mm Solothurn light machine gun, produced under license in Hungary. The Hungarians also captured significant amount of Slovakian, Yugoslavian and Polish light machine guns with ammunition. The disarmed Polish Forces had 344 wz. 26 (BAR) and 60 French and 69 German light machine guns. The Hungarian captured 300 Czeh, 189 Romanian and 235 Serbian vz. 26 light machine guns. Plus 120 French WW1 and 180 German Maxim light machine guns were taken from the Yugoslavian Army. The captured light machine guns were pressed into service at the second line units or given to the Police and Gendarmerie Forces.

24/43 M. 7.9mm Mandsen light machine guns

The Madsen light machine gun was adopted by the Royal Danish Army in 1902. It was the world's first true light machine gun produced in quantity. It was expansive to produce, but reliable, despite the very complicated mechanism. Early 20s the Hungarians purchased the 7.9mm Mandsen machine guns as the 24 M. light machine gun. It was in service until 1931, replaced by the 31 M. light machine gun. In 1943, to ease the weapon shortage, the Hungarians purchased 2000 Mandsen light machine guns, named 43 M.

Technical characteristics

Country of origin	Dannish
Specification	24/43 M. light machine gun
Manufacturer	Madsen
Calibre	7,92mm
Weight	9,07 kg
Length	1150mm
Barrell length	475mm
Magazine	30 rounds
Muzzle velocity	715 m/s
Range	1900m
Rate of fire	350 rounds/minute

31 M. 8mm light machine gun

The *Maschinengewehr* 30, or MG 30 was a German-designed light machine gun in the 1930s. Rheinmetall Factory circumvented the provisions of the peace treaty and outsourcing the production to the Swiss manufacturer Waffenfabrik Solothurn. In accordance with the modernisation of the Hungarian Army 2000–3000 was purchased and put into service as Solothurn *31 M.* light machine gun. The FÉG factory in Budapest prepared for serial production under its license, between 1931 and 1938, a few hundred were produced each year. The gun is an air-cooled, recoil-operated design and featuring a rapid barrel-change system introduced to facilitate prolonged firing from an air-cooled gun. However, the side-mounted 25-rounds curved box magazine only produced a rate of fire of 350 shots per minute. It had a bipod, in 1938 the mounting system was upgraded, got a solid tripod 38 M. heavy mount, which able the 31 M. light machine gun to deliver more precise fire and used for platoon/company level A/A weapon too. From 1938 to 1944 Danuvia Factory produced 9033 31 M. light machine guns.

Technical characteristics

Country of origin	Switzerland/Hungary
Specification	31 M. light machine gun
Manufacturer	FÉG
Calibre	8mm 8X56 R
Weight	9,5 kg
Length	1162mm
Barrell length	600mm
Magazine	25 rounds
Muzzle velocity	761 m/s
Range	2000 meters
Rate of fire	350 rounds/minute

34 M. and 42 M. 7,9mm light machine guns

The MG 34 is a German recoil-operated air-cooled general-purpose machine gun, first tested in 1929, introduced in 1934, and issued to units in 1936. It introduced an entirely new concept in automatic firepower – universal machine gun – and is generally considered the world's first general-purpose machine gun. Its combination of exceptional mobility – being light enough to be carried by one man – and high rate of fire (of up to 900 rounds per minute) was unmatched. However, the MG 34 did have some problems. An example of this is that the MG 34 broke down easily if it got dust on it. It was also quite expensive to make. In 1944 the Germans handed over 2000 MG34/34 M. light machine gun to the Hungarian fighting units. The MG 42 was a general-purpose machine gun. The MG 42 was designed to improve the M 34, it known for being reliable, simple and easy to use. However, it is best known for its very high rate of fire.
At the end of the war unknown number of 7.9mm 42 M. light/medium machine guns (depends on the bipod or tripod system) put into Hungarian service.

Technical characteristics

Country of origin	Germany	Germany
Specification	34 M. light machine gun	42 M. light/medium machine gun
Manufacturer	Rheinmetall-Borsig AG	Mauser Werke AG
Calibre	7,92mm Mauser	7,92mm Mauser
Weight	12 kg, 32 kg with tripod	11,5 kg
Length	1219mm	1220mm
Magazine	50-250 rounds in drum or belt	50-250 rounds belt
Muzzle velocity	765 m/s	755 m/s
Range	2000 meters	3000 meters
Rate of fire	800-900 round/minutes	1200-1500 rounds/minute

▲ Hungarian officer posing with PPS submachine gun, having German MP-40 magazine pouch. (Deák)

At right: Hungarian dispatchriders on BMW R-75 sidecar motorbike armed with 43 M. submachine gun, belonged to the Hussar Division, 1944. (Illésfalvi)

▲ The 31 M. light machine gun got tripod in 1938, which enabled it to produce a more accurate fire on land target as well as act as an anti-aircraft role with special sight. However, the magazine capacity and the rate of fire did not make it suitable for this task. (Fortepan)

▲ From the mid-30s the 8mm 31 M. Solothurn light machine gun become the standard automata weapon, behind the gunner a Puch G350 motorbike is visible. (Fortepan/Ladinek)

▼ Soldiers posing with their 31 M. light machine gun, 39 M. submachine gun, 35 M. rifles. The light machine gunner is a career NCO, the two soldiers in the back wearing the distinctive field cap with feather of the field gendarme. (Deák)

▲ At the bicycle troops the 31 M. light machine gun was transported by the sturdy 32 M. military bicycle, manufactured by the Weiss Mandréd Factory. (Mujzer)

▲ The standard machine gun of the Hungarian Army was the 8mm 07/31 M. Schwarzlose, originated from the Austro-Hungarian Army, modernised and produced by the Hungarians. The machine gun had a distinctive flash hider, not always applied on the weapons. (Fortepan/Horváth)

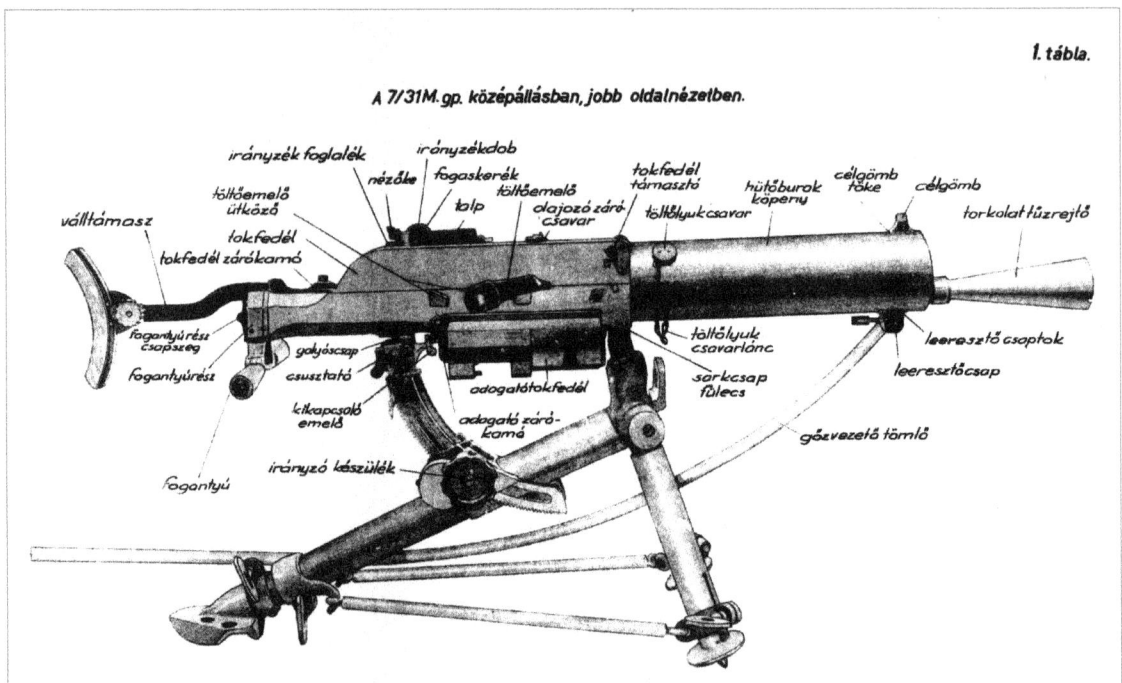

▲ The 07/31 M. Schwarzlose 8mm machine gun, The standard machine gun of the Hungarians also inherited from the K. und K. Armee of WW1, ,according to the picture the machine gun has a shoulder stock which normaly was not used. (Service Manual)

MACHINE GUNS

The machine gun is a fully automatic firearm designed for sustained direct fire with rifle cartridges. The first successful weapon was the Maxim machine gun, used the recoil power of the previously fired bullet to, enabling a much higher rate of fire. Maxim also introduced the use of water cooling, via a water jacket around the barrel, to reduce overheating. The WW1 machine guns mostly were bulky, sturdy and heavy pieces, normally put on tripod with water jacket. Beside the standard Schwarzlose machine gun, the Hungarians also captured and pressed into service significant amount of Slovakian, Yugoslavian and Polish machine guns with ammunition. The Slovaks had Czeh 7,92mm vz. 37 and rechambered Schwarlose machine guns, altogether around 120 were captured. The Serbs beside WW1 French and German machine guns, kept the 8mm and the rechambered Schwarzlose weapons. From Yugoslavian stocks 500 machine guns arrived at Hungary. The disarmed Polish forces also had 7,92mm wz. 30 Browning, WW1 German and French machine guns, altogether 350 pieces.

07/31 M. Schwarzlose 8mm machine gun

The standard machine gun of the Hungarians also inherited from the K. und K. Armee of WW1.
The 8mm 07/31 M. Schwarzlose machine gun was the only machine gun employing the retarded blow-back system the gun was very heavy and solid and due to the blow-back mechanism a short barrel fitted with a flash hider. The Schwarzlose was a belt-fed machine gun, usually mounted on a tripod, it was water-cooled barrel, internally the weapon was comparatively inexpensive to manufacture. It's unusual, delayed blowback mechanism contained only a single spring. The initial variants had a cyclic rate of about 400 rounds/minute. During World War I this was increased to 580 rounds/minute by using a stronger mainspring. The Schwarzlose was robust and reliable, if used in its intended role as an infantry support weapon. It had an armour shield to protect the crew. The machine gun was transported by mules in two loads: barrel system and tripod. In firing position, it weighed 40 kilograms. In 1931 the machine gun was re-barrelled to fire the new 31 M. cartridges. The machine gun got a special anti-aircraft tripod and sight, however, due its low rate of fire it was totally inadequate for this role. The 07/31 M. Schwarzlose machine guns were produced by the FÉG in Hungary until 1944. From 1938 until 1944 2464 Schwarzlose machine gun was produced in Hungary. By the end of the war gap stop machine guns were used, utilising the 8mm 37/a M. armoured vehicles' machine gun on improvised tripods.

Technical characteristics

Country of origin	Austro-Hungary
Specification	07/31 M. machine gun
Manufacturer	Steyer/FÉG
Calibre	8mm 8X56 R
Weight	41,4 kg with tripod
Length	950mm
Barrel length	530mm
Magazine	250 rounds belt
Muzzle velocity	625 m/s
Range	3500 meters
Rate of fire	350 rounds/minute
Crew	5

▲ Photo on the left, 31 M. light machine gun in firing position on fixed mount, attached to a Krupp Protze all-trerain truck. Photo on the right: Reconnaissance troops armed with 31 M. light machine gun and 35 M. rifles next to a 39 M. Csaba armoured car in 1941. Large photo: Troops armed with 07/31 M. machine gun, MP-40 submachine gun in Hungary, winter of 1944.

▲ The 07/31 M. machine guns belonged to the machine gun companies of the infantry and cavalry units, providing fire support, even due to its range it was used for indirect fire support too. (Mujzer)

▼ An artistic photo about the 07/31 M. machine gun on anti-aircraft tripod with sight, it was hopelessly inadequate against aircrafts due to its low rate of fire. (Fortepan/Konok)

▲ The Hungarians captured significant number light machine guns in the early stage of the war, the 7,92mm vz. 26 Zbrojovka light machine guns were issued to the combat support, support and second line unit. (Author's collection)

▲ Infantry squad carry out the maintenance of their weapons, 31 M. light machine gun and 35 M. rifles during the preparations to take back Transylvania from Romania. (Fortepan/Kókány)

▲ The motorised rifle battalions' machine gun companies transported their Schwarzlose machine guns on Krupp Protze half squad trucks, on tripod, 4th Motorised Rifle Battalion, summer of 1941, Ukraine. (ECPA)

▼ Soldiers firing with the 20 mm Solothurn 36 M. anti-tank rifle.

▲ The Hungarians also used captured Soviet 7,62mm M1910 Maxim machine gun on two wheels Sokolov mount and shield.at the River Don in summer of 1942. (Author's collection)

▲ The Hungarian occupation forces were also armed with 7,92mm MG 08 Maxim machine gun to protect the railway lines in Ukraine. (Deák)

HAND AND RIFLE GRENADES

The grenade is a small explosive weapon typically thrown by hand, but can also shot from the muzzle of a rifle or a grenade launcher. The Hungarian troops met with hand and rifle grenades in WW1. During WW2, the Hungarian Army used several types of hand grenades and rifle grenades. The Hungarian industry produced the homemade 31 M., 36 M. Vécsey hand grenades, 38/a M. flame grenades, 42 M. hand and 43 M. smoke or flesh grenades. The troops also used German 29 M. eggs and 24 M., 42 M. stick grenades.

31 M. hand grenade
In 1931, a small, hand grenade without a handle was introduced by the Army to replace the World War I stick grenades and their improved versions. The 31 M. grenades, however, had many problems, which eventually necessitated the introduction of new types. After unscrewing the transport fuse, releasing the carry fuse and dropping the ejection fuse in flight, the grenade is detonated on impact by an impact detonator. Its major disadvantage is that it cannot be armed in the hand and therefore has limited use in street fighting and no use at all against combat vehicles. In the late 1930s, the type was replaced by the 36 M. Vécsey hand grenade.

36 M. hand grenade
However, there were many problems with the 31 M. grenades, which eventually made it necessary to introduce new types, the 36 M. and the 37 M. (Demeter) hand grenades designed by Captain Zoltán Vécsey. The new grenades were introduced in 1937 and tested in 1938, but the existing 31 M. hand grenades were kept. The Army ordered the Vécsey and Demeter hand grenades, both with percussion fuses in equal shares. However, the Demeter had the disadvantage of the chemical fuse, difficult to storage. Mainly in foreign literature the 36 M. is compared with Italian models of similar appearance, e.g. the Mod. 35 hand grenade, suggesting that the Hungarian grenade would have Italian antecedents. The early hand grenade types of the Hungarian Army, the 31 M., 36 M. (Vécsey) and 37 M. (Demeter) were not equipped with a delayed fuse. They exploded on impact, which had several advantages: they could not be thrown back by the enemy; they did not roll when thrown on sloping or vertical surfaces; and, as was found during the war, they were suitable for close combat. However, they also had their drawbacks. These characteristics made them ill-suited fighting in forested terrain, or for fighting armoured vehicles or in localities where the grenade had to be thrown through a window or hatch.

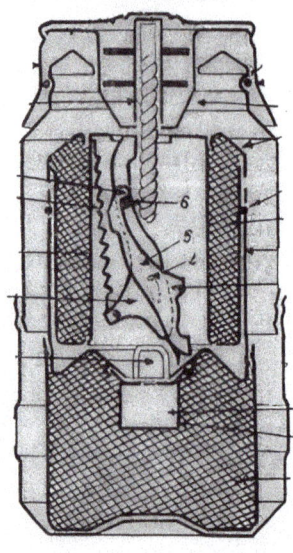

▲ At the beginning of the war, the 36 M. Vécsey hand grenade was the standard hand grenade. (Service manual). At right: Photo of the 36 M. Vécsey hand grenade secured for transportation. (Regia Militia Hungarorum)

42 M. hand grenade

The designer of the 36 M. hand grenade, Captain Zoltán Vécsey, presented his grenade in 1942, which was made according to the new requirements based on the German experiences and developments. It was a delay fuse hand grenade, put into production the following year, but it was only in 1944 that the troops received it in larger numbers. the 42 M. hand grenade had wooden handle and tinplate headstock. Although it also uses a timing fuse, its design and operating principle is different from that of the German grenade. The fuse, located in a tube at the end of the handle and extending into the cavity of the headstock, is not activated by a drawstring striker like at the German stick grenade, but by a striking pin which is pulled by the momentum of the throw and then returned by a spring which is pushed into the hammer handle.

Technical characteristics

Country	Hungary	Hungary	Hungary
Specification	31 M. hand grenade	36 M. hand grenade	42 M. stick grenade
Manufacturer	Krolupper	different companies	Elzet, Krolupper
Weight		250gr	344 gr
Explosive		85gr	120 gr
Fuse		34 M.	34a/M.
Blast radius		5-10 meter	5-10 meters

38/a-39/a M. M. flame grenade

Three types of flame grenades were designed for fighting on built-up areas. The flame grenade was introduced on 27 September 1938. It was a short-necked glass cylinder filled with petrol or motor spirit, in the lower part of which (in a small recess) a separate glass ampoule was fitted from the outside and filled with a chemical substance which ignited immediately on contact with air. Length: 180 mm, diameter: 77 mm, barrel length: 193 mm, diameter: 107 mm. The bottle of the friction-ignition flame grenade contained 2/3 petrol and 1/3 flame-spraying oil. The makeshift flame grenade/Molotov cocktail was a simple glass bottle filled with a highly flammable liquid.

43 M. smoke grenade

Primarily intended to blind enemy tanks, the fog acid that entered the vehicle's enclosed space could also act as an irritant. A sealed, pear-shaped glass grenade body without a primer, filled with fulminating acid up to about two fingers below the neck. The remaining approximately 12 % air is used to compensate for pressure fluctuations due to changes in external temperature.

Technical characteristics

Country	Hungary	Hungary	Hungary
Specification	38/a-39/a M. flame grenade	43 M. smoke/stun grenade	43 M. stunt grenade
Manufacturer		Mercure Rt. Chemical Factory	
Weight	0,6 kg	0,71 kg	
Explosive	0,5l benzoin	290 cm3 fog acid	

39 M. egg grenade

The Model 39 "egg hand grenade" was a German fragmentation hand grenade introduced in 1939. The offensive high explosive version was considered extremely ineffective in comparison to the standard stick grenade models. The defensive fragmentation version of the grenade had a fragmentation sleeve wrapped around the exterior of the grenade, which would turn into high-speed shrapnel when the grenade exploded, giving it a longer range and greater damage ability to the enemy but also include the thrower in the danger zone.

24 M. stick grenade
The M24 was beside the more common Model 39 grenade, the standard hand grenade of the German Wehrmacht during World War II. The Model 1924 was rather ineffective by itself at damaging or disabling an enemy armoured vehicle or destroying fortifications. It also lacked the shrapnel effect of most other grenades of the time. A common solution was an improvised "bundle charge". The heads of several M24 grenades – their handles and fuses removed – would be strapped around a complete grenade. However, the added weight made it more difficult to throw, and the increased size meant that it was not practical to carry with one hand and that far fewer could be carried.

43 M. stick grenade
The Model 1924 grenade was technically "succeeded" by the Model 1943 (M43). This was a copy with a few expensive parts removed or replaced for easier production – and because of this, the original remained in service with Wehrmacht infantry right to the end of the war. The only significant alterations in the M43's design was the inclusion of a self-contained detonator, meaning that the fuse and the explosive were directly linked. The M43 also utilized an entirely different fuse assembly, very similar to that of the Model 39 grenade. Not only was the stick no longer needed to be hollowed out for a pull cord as in the M24, minimizing the amount of woodworking required to manufacture each grenade, it also made the stick optional so it could replace the Model 39 as the thrower could choose in which configuration to use the grenade.
The Hungarian troops were normally supplied with German hand grenades on the frontline to resupply the used stocks.

Technical characteristics

Country	German	Germany	Germany
Specification	39 M. egg grenade	24 M. stick grenade	42 M. stick grenade
Weight	298 gr	500 gr	500 gr
Explosive	120 gr	180 gr	160 gr
Fuse	B.Z.E. 39	B.Z.24, B.Z.E.39	
Blast radius	5-10 meters	15 meters	5-10 meters

Rifle grenades
The Hungarians also used rifle grenades, which was fired from the barrel fitting or trumpet mounted on the muzzle of the rifle. The cartridge was like a blank cartridge, with no projectile in the case. The rifle grenade was a steep-trajectory weapon used beyond the range of the hand grenade, between 25 and 150 m. The rifle grenade was intended to use as a replacement for the 1936 M. anti-tank rifle, for fire support of the infantry squads, engaging tanks and armoured fighting vehicles. In mid-1943, Hungary acquired from the Germans the Bergmann fragmentation grenade, the production rights for the trumpet and the sight system, and in the second half of the year the armour-piercing grenade. Until the start of domestic mass production, 200,000 rifle grenades with 500 trumpets were ordered from Germany. With the start of domestic production in January 1944, 50,000 rifle grenades were produced each month.

Technical characteristics

Country of origin	Germany	Germany
Specification	Rifle grenade	Rifle anti-tank grenade
Overall weight	0,255 kg	0,25 kg
Explosion weight	0,3 kg	0,5 kg
Range	90 meters	45 meters
Blast radius	10 meters	13 meters
Armour penetration		20mm

▲ At left: The German 42 M. stick grenade was issued to the Hungarian troops in large quantity from 1942, on the front line. On this staged photo the soldier carries light machine gun and machine gun belts, however we have to note that the 31 M. light machine gun was not belt fed, it had magazine. (War Correspondent Company)

At right: From the second half of the war a newly designed 42 M. Vécsey hand grenade was put into service; the grenades could screw together to improve the blast effect. (Szollár)

▲ The 38 M. flame grenades were development to blind the loopholes and observation devices of the enemy bunkers and to use as incendiary device. The stormtrooper hava one grenade in metal transport carrier attached to his belt. (Mujzer)

LAND MINES

The land mine is an explosive weapon concealed under or camouflaged on the ground, and designed to destroy or disable enemy targets, ranging from combatants to vehicles and tanks, as they pass over or near it. The Hungarian Army developed and used a wide variety of anti-personal and anti-tank mines during the war, home designs, German and captured explosives too. Home-made 36 M. tripwire, and plate mines, 43 M. tripwire and 43 M. bouncing mines and brick mines belonged to the engineers.

36 M. TAK. plate mine

The plate mine, introduced in 1936 by the Hungarian Army, was a witty attempt to combine infantry and tank mines into a single weapon. But, as is often the case, the hybrid solution ultimately failed to serve either purpose in practice: the one-and-a-half-kilogram charge proved unnecessarily large against infantry, but insufficient against tanks. Transportation: one pack of 6 stacked 36 M. Tak. and a box containing 6 36 M. mine lighters form a Tak. package, held together by a hemp strap passed through the cut-outs in the mine covers. 5 of these Tak. packs, i.e. 30 mines and 30 fuses, are placed in a Tak. box.

43 M. TAK. cumulative anti-tank mine

Major József Misnay, who served at the HTI, during experimentations with charges invented the cumulative effect. It was named as Misnay–Schardin effect, or platter effect, is a characteristic of the detonation of a broad sheet of explosive. No exact date is known, but in 1942 a lecture was given by Misnay about the shape charges. The shaped or cumulative charge is an explosive charge shaped to focus the effect of the explosive›s energy. That time it was revolutionary development of using the cumulative effect of the charge. The exact armour penetration is unknown. It was used for booby-traps and observed explosive charge to. In April 1944, already 16000 43 M. TAK. reached the troops and the manufacturing was planned 12000/month.

44 M. LÖTAK anti-tank mine

Based on the cumulative anti-tank mine a launchable version was designed to penetrate the side armour of the armoured vehicles. Unfortunately, neither a copy nor a technical description of it has survived. What is certain is that they were used in Transylvania to close the passes, and before 15 October 1944 they were also used to close the castle; The forward-looking nature of the weapon is underlined by the fact that French and German experts were not able to produce a similar weapon until the 1960s. It was effective against essentially all armour, and was made of wood, paper, plastic (bakelite) and canvas, so it was not easy to detect.

Technical characteristics

Country of origin	Hungary	Hungary	
Specification	36 M. TAK. plate anti-tank mine	43 M. TAK. anti-tank cumulative mine	44 M. Lötak
Weight	3,5 kg	5,64 kg	5,64 kg
Diameter	25 cm	30,8 cm	30,8 cm
Explosive charge	1,5 kg Tri. II	4,42 kg	4,42 kg
Fuse	36 M. mine fuse	43 M. TAK.	

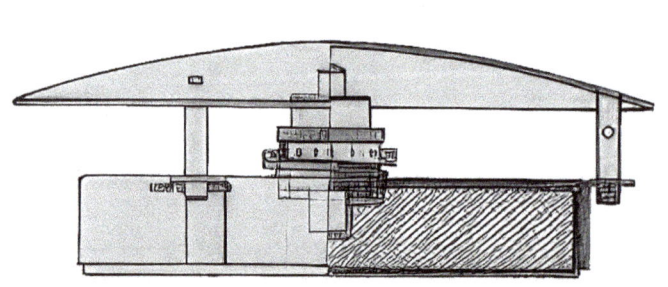 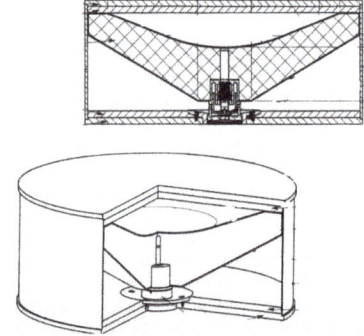

▲ Left: The technical drawings of the 36 M. TAK. land/anti-tank plate mine. (Technical Manual). Right: Technical drawings of the 43 M. TAK. cumulative anti-tank mine. (Technical Manual)

INFANTRY HEAVY WEAPONS

LIGHT MORTARS

Based on the lessons of the WW1 the infantry platoons, companies fire power was improved with light mortars about 50mm Calibre. Its intended role was to engage pockets of resistance that were beyond a hand grenade's throwing range. These light weighted weapons were carried in combat by the crew of two, plus the ammunition bearers, providing fire support beyond the range of the hand grenades against targets behind cover.

39 M. 50mm light mortar

To improve the fire power of the infantry, a company-level light mortar was invented by the FÉG Factory. The home design 39 M. 50mm light mortar was intended to deploy at the rifle companies' heavy weapon platoons. The platoons had two 39 M. light mortar and two 36M, anti-tank rifle squads, armed with two-two 39 M. light mortars and 36 M. anti-tank rifles. The FÉG Factory manufactured 826 light mortars from 1938 until 1944. The weapon was too heavy comparing with the rifle grenades and it allotted ammunition was too few.

GRW 36 50mm light mortar

The mortar's development was started in 1934 by Rheinmetall-Borsig AG and it was adopted for service in 1936. Until 1938, it used a complicated telescopic sight. By 1941, the Granatwerfer 36 was seen as too complex for its intended role, the shell was too light and the range too short. It was used as a platoon mortar and operated by a 3-man team. In the summer of 1942, according to the Hungarian German arms deal, the 2nd Hungarian Army was supplemented with 171 German 36M 50mm light mortars.

Technical characteristics

Country of origin	Hungary	Germany
Specification	39 M. light mortar	GRW 36 50mm light mortar
Manufacturer	FÉG	Rheinmetall
Calibre	50mm	50mm
Barrell weight	410mm	465mm
Weight	20 kg	20 kg
Projectile weight	845 g	9 g
Muzzle velocity	90 m/s	75 m/s
Rate of fire	22 rounds/minute	15-25 rounds/minute
Range	50-860 meters	60-520 meters
Transportation	carried by the crew	carried by the crew
Crew	2+ ammunition handlers	2+ ammunition handlers

MORTARS

Mortars are typically used as indirect fire weapons for close fire support with a variety of ammunition. The typical mortar of the 30-40s was a simple muzzle-loaded weapon, consisting of a smoothbore metal tube fixed to a base plate with a lightweight bipod mount. The medium mortars at the beginning of the war used for battalion level fire support.

36 M. and 36/39 M. 81mm mortar

The battalion level medium mortar of the troops was the 81mm 36M mortar. It entered into service in 1936. Later it was modified as 36/39 M. mortar with improved range of 6200 meters. The mortar was transported in three parts. It was the best battalion level heavy weapon of the troops. At the beginnings only two medium mortars were allocated to the battalions heavy/machine gun companies and four to the regimental mortar companies. From 1942, the battalions' heavy companies had a mortar platoon with four mortars and the infantry regiments mortar companies had six mortars. Altogether 1166 mortars were produced from 1941 until

1944. The Hungarians struggling with the shortfall of medium mortars. The Germans supplied them with German Granatwerfer 34 as well as with captured weapons. From Dutch stocks about 150 plus some Czeh and Yugoslavian mortars were put into Hungarian service. The Hungarians, just like the Germans utilised the captured Soviet 82mm mortar shells, which fitted into the 81,4mm Hungarian and German mortars.

34 M. 80mm mortar

The 8 cm Granatwerfer 34 was the standard German infantry mortar throughout World War II. It was noted for its accuracy and rapid rate of fire. The weapon was of conventional design and broke down into three loads (smooth bore barrel, bipod, baseplate) for transport. Attached to the bipod were a traversing handwheel and a cross-levelling handwheel below the elevating mechanism. A panoramic sight was mounted on the traversing mechanism yoke for fine adjustments. The mortar employed conventional 8 cm 3.5 kg shells (high explosive or smoke) with percussion fuses. The range could be extended by fitting up to three additional powder charges between the shell tailfins. The Germans handed over 37 mortars to 2nd Hungarian Army until January 1943. There were negotiations to provide 8-8 Dutch origin 81mm mortar for the infantry regiments of the Hungarians.

Technical characteristics

Country of origin	Hungary	German	Dutch
Specification	36 M. 81mm mortar	GrW 34 81mm mortar	Stokes / Brandt 81 mm mortar
Manufacturer	DIMÁVAG	Rheinmetall	
Calibre	81,4mm	81,4mm	81,4mm
Barrel length	1215mm	1143mm	1110-1260mm
Weight	85 kg	62-75 kg	56 kg
Projectile weight	4kg	3,5 kg	3,25-6,5 kg
Rate of fire	20-25 rounds/minute	15-25 rounds/minute	18 rounds/minute
Muzzle velocity	174 m/s	174 m/s	174 m/s
Range	50-4000 meters	400-2400 meters	1200-2800
Towing	horse-drawn, motorised	horse-drawn, motorised	horse-drawn, motorised
Crew	5-7	5	3

▲ Camouflaged Hungarian 36 M. mortar in a firing position in a deep ravine at the River Don in summer of 1942. (War Correspondent Company)

▲ From 1941, the infantry companies were supported by two 50mm 39 M. FÉG light mortars, the projectiles were carried in metal boxes contained six grenades. (Author's collection)

▼ Mortar men managing the sight of the 81,4mm 36 M. mortar, the tube is at low angel to achieve long range. (Author's collection)

▲ The 81,4mm 36 M. mortar was the standard fire support weapon of the infantry battalions. On the picture reserve officer cadets manning the mortar on an exercise. (Author's collection)

▲ The Germans handed over to the 2nd Hungarian Army GRW 36 light mortars, for the heavy weapon platoons of the infantry companies. The German ammunition box contained eight grenades. (War Correspondent Company)

43 M. 120mm heavy mortar

Developed in 1942, the 12 cm GrW 42 was an attempt to give German infantry units a close support weapon with greater performance than the mortars used in general service at the time. This weapon was very similar to the M1938 mortar used by Soviet forces on the Eastern Front which in turn was an improved version of the French 120 mm Brandt Mle 1935 mortar. The GrW 42 was basically the usual three-part construction made up of a circular base plate like the previous Soviet design, the tube itself and the supporting bipod. Because of the greater weight of the weapon (280 kilograms or 620 pounds) a two-wheeled axle was utilized, enabling the mortar to be towed into action. The axle could then be quickly removed before firing. The Hungarians supplied by license production of the German Granatwerfer 42 mortars in 1944. By the end of the war 200 were manufactured and handed over to the Hungarian troops, the plan was to equip the regimental mortar companies with these weapons.

Technical characteristics

Country of origin	German
Specification	43 M. 120mm heavy mortar
Manufacturer	MÁVAG
Calibre	120mm
Weight	280 kg
Projectile weight	15,6 kg
Muzzle velocity	280 m/s
Rate of fire	8-10 rounds/minute
Range	6 km
Towing	motorised

▲ A rare photo of the German 120 mm heavy mortar in Hungarian service, probably taken on a German conversion training held for the Hungarians in 1944. (Author's collection)

ANTI-TANK RIFLE

The anti-tank rifles are designed to penetrate the armour of armoured vehicles. To be able for the intended role, the anti-tank rifles had larger calibre and greater muzzle velocity than the normal rifles, in return their weight and size were also bigger. The first anti-tank rifle of 7,92mm was developed by the German in World War I, to counter the Allied tanks.

36 M. 20mm anti-tank rifle

The company-level anti-tank weapon was the 36 M. 20mm anti-tank rifle, produced in Hungary under license from Solothurn, Switzerland. It was recoil-operated to give semiautomatic fire and had a well-padded shoulder–piece above a rear monopod, a combination which managed to absorb much of the recoil force. It fired a base-fused armour-piercing shell. It was a powerful anti-tank weapon of the 1930s but was outdated by 1941. It was mainly used for close fire support at rifle company level. It was heavy and difficult to move in combat. The strong recoil requested well-built gunners. It was transported by a cart, horse pack, vehicles, even on the sidecar of the motor bicycle. The Toldi light tanks and Csaba armoured cars were also armed with the same weapon. In Hungary 1911 anti-tank rifles were manufactured from 1938 until 1944.

Technical characteristics

Country of origin	Switzerland
Specification	36 M. 20mm anti-tank rifle
Manufacturer	Solothurn/Danuvia
Calibre	20mm 20x105B
Weight	45 kg
Projectile weight	337 gr AP
Muzzle velocity	762 m/s
Rate of fire	30-35 rounds/minute
Range	2000 meters
Armour penetration	15-18mm at 300 meters
Towing	horse-drawn two wheeled chart, motorised
Crew	2, gunner and loader plus ammunition carriers

▲ Mortar team exercising with the 81,4mm 36 M. mortar, the crew were only armed with service pistols, which were insufficient in combat situation. (Mujzer)

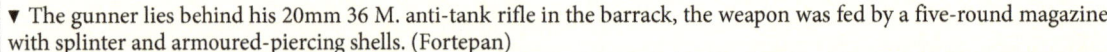

▲ Two men crew of the 20mm 36 M. anti-tank rifle in a firing position on the bank of a small river, the loader lies behind a metal ammunition box, holding his 37 M. pistol. (Mujzer)

▼ The gunner lies behind his 20mm 36 M. anti-tank rifle in the barrack, the weapon was fed by a five-round magazine with splinter and armoured-piercing shells. (Fortepan)

HANDHELD ROCKET-PROPELLED ANTI-TANK WEAPONS

From early 1944, the Hungarians were armed with German-made Faustpatrone called Panzerfaust and with reloadable 88mm schwere Raketenpanzerbüchse 54 called Panzerschreck. The Germans also supplied the Raketenwerfer 43 "Püppchen", the towed version of the Panzerschreck in May 1944. The Hungarians also manufactured the 60mm version of the Panzerschreck as 44 M. hand-held anti-tank rocket launcher, supplied the troops by mid-1944.

Panzerfaust 43

The Panzerfaust was a single-shot man-portable anti-tank systems developed by the Germans during World War II. The Panzerfaust-design consisted of a light recoilless launcher tube outfitted with a single pre-loaded high-explosive anti-tank warhead protruding from the muzzle. It was an inexpensive, easy-to-use anti-tank weapon for the common infantry man, operated by a single soldier. Firing was done from under the arm at an upward angle as the effective firing range was barely beyond that of hand grenades (30–60 m (98–197 ft) max). After use the launcher was discarded. Different versions were produced; Faustpatron 30, 60, 100 and 150, these differed from each other in size, range and warhead. The first Hungarian troops were issued with the Faustpatrons in spring of 1944, on the Eastern Front, Galicia to counter the lack of heavy anti-tank guns at the troops.

Raketenpanzerbüchse 54

Panzerschreck was the popular name for the Raketenpanzerbüchse 54, an 88 mm reusable anti-tank rocket launcher developed by Germany in World War II. The Panzerschreck was designed as a lightweight infantry anti-tank weapon and was an enlarged copy of the American bazooka.[4] The weapon was shoulder-launched and fired a fin-stabilized rocket with a shaped-charge warhead. It was made in smaller numbers than the Panzerfaust. Calibre 88 mm was selected as the existing RPzB. Gr. 4312 for 8.8 cm Raketenwerfer 43 was reused for Panzerschreck. Warhead and fusing were carried over, but the rocket motor's housing needed lengthening to accommodate the longer rocket motor. It had a blast shield to protect the operator due to the heavy blast heat and smoke. The Hungarians got the first Panzerschreks in the summer of 1944, in Galicia and used until the very end of the war.

Technical characteristics

Country of origin	Germany	Germany	Germany
Specification	Panzerfaust 43	Raketenpanzerbüchse 54	Raketenwerfer 43
Manufacturer	HASAG		WASAG
Calibre		88mm	88mm
Length	100 cm	164 cm	297 cm
Weight	2,3-7 kg	11 kg	143 kg
Projectile weight	400g -2900 gr	2,6 kg	2,6 kg
Muzzle velocity	28-85 m/s	110 m/s	110 m/s
Range	60 meters	150 meters	500 meters
Armour penetration	140-320mm	95-230mm	160mm
Towing	man portable	man portable	pack, motorised
Crew	1	2	

44 M. 60mm anti-tank rocket launcher

The Hungarian 44 M. handheld anti-tank rocket launcher was inspired by the German 88mm anti-tank rocket launcher. The Hungarian acknowledged the success of the German weapon, which among other anti-tank rockets improved significantly the anti-tank capabilities of the infantry in return of low costs, simple training and use. The Hungarian reduced the calibre from 88 to 60mm, which gave better ballistic characteristics. The Hungarians used the 44 M. armour piercing rocket, which in fact was cumulative charge. The weapon was distributed among the troops in second half of 1944. The Guard Rifle Battalion, which protected the Castle and the Governor of Hungary, Admiral Miklós Horthy was also equipped with the rocket launchers.

▲ The Hungarians also got the Raketenpanzerbüchse 54 in 1944, the Panzersrceht 88 mm reusable anti-tank rocket launcher and the Panzerfaust used together in tank-hunter teams. (Author's collaction)

▼ At the end of the war the Hungarians developed their own reusable 60 mm 44 M. anti-tank rocket launcher, crewed by two, gunner and ammunition handler. (Sárhidai)

▲ The troops of the 1st Cavalry/Hussar Division were armed with handheld Panzerfaust 43 anti-tank rockets. Two Hussars manning its position armed with 31 M. light machine gun, stick grenades and Panzerfaust. (Széplaki)

▼ The Troops of the 1st Army was issued with hand-held 43 M. anti-tank rocket in spring 1944, Galícia. Training courses were held behind the front inspected by General Beregffy. (War Correspondent Company)

Technical characteristics

Country of origin	Hungary
Specification	44 M. 60mm anti-tank rocket launcher
Manufacturer	unknown
Calibre	60mm
Weight	10 kg
Lenght	180 cm
Projectile weight	2,55 kg
Muzzle velocity	80 m/s
Range	60-150 meters
Armour penetration	100mm
Towing	man portable
Crew	2

Flame throwers

A flamethrower is a ranged incendiary device designed to project a controllable jet of fire. Modern flamethrowers were first used during the trench warfare conditions of WW1 and their use greatly increased in WW2. It can be vehicle-mounted, as on a tank, or man-portable.

Based on the WW1 experiences, the Italian WW1 Lancia flamethrowers were used by the the grenadier and jager units as well as the engineer troops. used Italian WW1 Lancia flame throwers. Later 41M and 43M portable flame throwers were used by storm troops and assault engineers.

Italian flamethrower

According to some sources Italian, Lancia portable flamethrowers served in the Hungarian Army. Due to the Italian Hungarian military cooperation, the CV35 tankette with flamethrower was presented, but not accepted in Hungary.

41 M. flamethrower

The Hungarians also designed their own portable flamethrower. High-pressure nitrogen was used to eject the combustible material from the tank. A device was used to ignite the liquid leaving the end of the flame-spraying tube in a spray-like manner. The length of the flame was adjusted by means of a control valve. The operator was protected by an asbestos suit and asbestos gloves. The 1941 M. flamethrower was 400 mm long, 600 mm wide and 250 mm high. Pressure in the cylinder was 30 atmospheres. Range 30 metres. A sustained fire lasted 10 to 12 seconds, and the two-barrel cylinder could expel 2 to 15 bursts of fire. On 21 November 1943, a new type of flamethrower, the 43 M. portable flamethrower, was introduced, but not manufactured until the end of war.

Technical characteristics

Country of origin	Italy		
Specification	Lancia flamethrower	41 M. flamethrower	43 M. flamethrower
Manufacturer			
Empty weight		14,7 kg	
Loaded weight		22 kg	
Flammable liquid		7 kg	
Range		30 meters	
Transportation			
Crew			

▲ The Hungarian storm troops and engineers used flamethrowers during the war. The operators used asbestos protective hood and suit against the heat. (War Correspondent Company)

▼ Hungarian storm engineer fought with portable flamethrower at the River Don in summer of 1942. (War Correspondent Company)

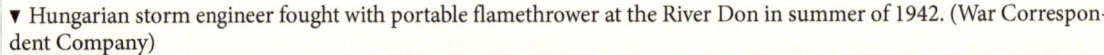

ANTI-TANK GUNS

Anti-tank gun is a form of artillery designed to destroy tanks and other armoured fighting vehicles, normally from a static defensive position. The development of specialized anti-tank munitions and anti-tank guns was prompted by the appearance of tanks during World War I. The anti-tank guns of the 1920s and 1930s were of small calibre; nearly all major armies possessing them used 37-40 M.m ammunition. As World War II progressed, the appearance of heavier tanks rendered these weapons obsolete, and anti-tank guns likewise began firing larger and more effective armour-piercing shells. Beside the standard ant-tank guns, the 2nd Hungarian Army used captured Soviet 45mm anti-tank guns at the River Don in 1942-1943.

36 M. 37mm anti-tank gun

Developed by Rheinmetall in 1933, it was first issued to the German Army in 1936, with 9,120 being available by the beginning of the war in September 1939 and a further 5,339 produced during the war. As the predominant anti-tank gun design in the world during the late 1930s, demand was high for the Pak 36, with another 6,000 examples produced for export and the design being copied by the Soviet Union as the 45mm anti-tank gun. Design of a horse-drawn, 37mm anti-tank gun (designated 37mm Pak L/45) by Rheinmetall commenced in 1924 and the first guns were issued in 1928. By the early 1930s, it was apparent that horse-drawn artillery was obsolescent, and the gun was modified for motorized transport by substituting magnesium-alloy wheels and pneumatic tires for the original spoked wooden wheels, allowing it to be towed at highway speeds. Redesignated the 37mm cm Pak 35/36, it began to replace the 37mm Pak L/45 in 1934 and first appeared in combat in 1936 during the Spanish Civil War. The Hungarians at the beginning of the war used the 36 M. 37mm anti-tank guns, purchased from Germany. At the Hungarian Army, the motorized version was towed by Krupp Protze light artillery tractor; the horsed version was drawn by two horses' gun limber. The Germans delivered the Pak 36 in 1937-1940 to the Hungarians. In 1941 four 36 M. anti-tank gun served at the infantry battalions, the infantry and cavalry regiments had one-one anti-tank gun companies with six guns. However, by 1941 the 37mm anti-tank guns were inferior against the medium and heavy tanks.

Technical characteristics

Country of origin	German
Specification	36 M. 37mm anti-tank gun
Manufacturer	Rheinmetall
Calibre	37mm L/45
Weight	328 kg
Projectile weight	354 gr. AP
Muzzle velocity	760 m/s
Range	5480 meters
Rate of fire	13 rounds/minute
Armour penetration	38 M.m at 360 meters
Gun shield	yes
Carriage	split trail
Towing	horse-drawn, motorised Krupp Protze truck
Crew	5

36 M. 37 mm Skoda anti-tank gun

The 3,7 cm KPÚV vz. 37 was an anti-tank gun produced by the Škoda Works that saw service in World War II. Originally designed for the Czechoslovak Army, some were also sold to Yugoslavia. The gun had a small shield and wooden-spoked wheels, although some were fitted with pneumatic wheels. The Hungarian Army captured several vz. 37 from the Slovak and Yugoslav Armies during the military operations in 1939 and 1941. From the captured 106 Yugoslavian anti-tank gun 65 were repaired, issued with Hungarian sight in June 1941 These anti-tank guns were repaired and supplied with the sight of the 36 M. anti-tank guns and put into service at the border guard and fortress battalion. In the summer of 1942, the Germans handed over 35 anti-tank guns to the 2nd Hungarian Army.

Technical characteristics

Country of origin	Czechoslovakia
Specification	36 M. 37mm anti-tank gun
Manufacturer	Skoda
Calibre	37mm L/47
Weight	370 kg
Projectile weight	800 gr. AP
Muzzle velocity	750 m/s
Range	1000-4000 meters
Rate of fire	12 rounds/minute
Armour penetration	37mm at 100, 26mm at 1000 meters
Gun shield	yes
Carriage	split trail
Towing	horse-drawn, motorised
Crew	5

36 M. 47mm anti-tank gun
The 47mm anti-tank gun Model 1931 was an artillery piece developed in 1931 for the Belgian Army which saw widespread service in the Battle of Belgium in 1940. There were two versions of the 47mm gun, each developed for a different situation. The infantry version and the light troops version. The infantry version was furnished with heavier but more durable full-rubber tires. In contrast, the light troops version was equipped with pneumatic tires for greater road mobility. Both versions were capable of being incorporated into fixed defences and bunkers for stationary purposes. With a total weight of 515 kilograms, not including ammunition or other equipment, the 47mm was a lot heavier than the German Pak 36. In 1942, the 2nd Hungarian Army was upgraded with 245 Belgian 47mm anti-tank guns captured by the Germans in 1940. The Belgian anti-tank guns were handed over without optical sights and spare parts with limited ammunition stocks. The guns were horsed drawn and ineffective against Soviet medium and heavy tanks.

Technical characteristics

Country of origin	Belgium
Specification	36 M. 47mmm anti-tank gun
Manufacturer	Fonderie Royal Autocannons
Calibre	47mm L/33
Weight	568 kg
Projectile weight	1,5 kg
Rate of fire	18-20 rounds/minute
Muzzle velocity	720 m/s
Range	1000-max 3000 meters
Armour penetration	64mm at 100/ 22mm at 1000 meters
Gun shield	yes
Carriage	split trail
Towing	horse drawn or motorised
Crew	7

▲ The German PAK 36, 36 M. 37mm anti-tank gun

▲ The Hungarians got their first anti-tank guns, the Pak 36/36 M. in late 30s. The first anti-tank guns were horse drawn with wooden spoked wheels. (Fortepan/Korner). At right: The mobile forces got the motorised version of the 36 M. anti-tank gun towed by Krupp Protze anti-tank tractors, the photo taken on 20 May 1937, during the visit of the Italian king in Hungary. (Fortepan/Ladinek)

◄ The Krupp Protze anti-tank gun tractor was built with Hungarian body used by the anti-tank platoons and companies of the mobile troops. (Fortepan/Horváth)

▲ Left: The Germans also handed over captured Belgian 47 mm anti-tank guns, designated as 36 M. to the 2nd Hungarian Army in 1942. (War Correspondent Company). Right: The captured vz. 37 Skoda anti-tank guns were repaired and pressed into service by the Hungarians, the fortress companies of the frontier guard battalion got the anti-tank guns in 1941. (Mujzer)

▼ Krupp Protze towing the 37 mm 36 M. anti-tank gun belonged to the Anti-tank Company of the 1st Motorised Rifle Battalion, during the bridgehead battles in summer of 1942, River Don. (War Correspondent Company)

▲ The German PAK 38, 38 M. 50mm anti-tank gun

38 M., Pak 38 50mm anti-tank gun

The Pak 38 (L/60) was a German anti-tank gun of 50 mm calibre. It was developed in 1938 by Rheinmetall-Borsig AG as a successor to the 37mm Pak 36, and was in turn followed by the 75mm Pak 40. The unique curved gun-shield design differed from most WWII anti-tank guns which had either one flat or two angled and one flat gun-shield plates for ease of manufacturing. The Pak 38 was first used by the German forces during the Second World War in April 1941. When the Germans faced Soviet tanks in 1941 during Operation Barbarossa starting June 1941, the Pak 38 was one of the few guns capable of penetrating the 45mm sloped armour of the T-34 medium tank at close range. The gun was also equipped with Panzergranate 40 APCR shots with a hard tungsten carbide core, in an attempt to penetrate the armour of the heavier KV-1 tank. The 2nd Hungarian Army got 54 Pak 38 anti-tank guns, two-two guns were assigned to the regimental anti-tank companies of the infantry regiments and the anti-tank companies of the motorized rifle battalions, towed by 38 M. Botond trucks. In late 1942, to replace the material losses 77 Pak 38 were handed over to the Hungarians.

Technical characteristics

Country of origin	German
Specification	38 M. 50mm anti-tank gun
Manufacturer	Rheinmetall-Borsig AG
Calibre	50mm L/60
Weight	1000 kg
Projectile weight	2,25 kg
Muzzle velocity	550-1300 m/s
Rate of fire	13 rounds/minutes
Range	2700 meters
Armour penetration	100mm at100/ 60mm at 1000 meters
Gun shield	yes
Carriage	split trail
Towing	motorised, 38 M. Botond truck
Crew	7

Pak 97/38 75mm anti-tank gun

The Pak97/38 was a typical stopgap German anti-tank gun used by the Wehrmacht in World War II. The gun was a combination of the barrel from the French Autocannon de 75 modèle 1897 fitted with a Swiss Solothurn muzzle brake and mounted on the carriage of the German 50mm Pak 38 and could fire captured French and Polish ammunition. Soon after the German invasion of the USSR in 1941, Wehrmacht units encountered new Soviet tanks, the medium T-34 and the heavy KV. The thick and/or sloped armour of these vehicles gave them invulnerability against German towed 37mm Pak 36 anti-tank guns. The situation led to requests for more powerful weapons that would be able to destroy them at normal combat ranges. Since Germany already had a suitable design, the 75mm Pak 40, this weapon entered production and the first pieces were delivered in November 1941. However, until enough of these were manufactured, some expedient solution was required. In the original configuration, those guns were ill-suited for fighting tanks because of their relatively low muzzle velocity, limited traverse (only 6°), and lack of a suitable suspension (which resulted in a transport speed of just 10–12 km/h). It was decided to solve the traverse and mobility problems by mounting the 75mm barrel on the modern split trail carriage of the 50mm Pak 38 anti-tank gun. To soften the recoil, the barrel was fitted with a large muzzle brake. The gun was primarily intended to use HEAT shells as the armour penetration of this type of ammunition does not depend on velocity. Together with light weight, good mobility and sufficient anti-armour performance with a HEAT shell, enough to penetrate T-34s in most situations; the side armour of the KV series could also be pierced, it made the gun a decent anti-tank weapon. It had shortcomings, particularly its low muzzle velocity. Although this did not affect the armour-piercing characteristics of its HEAT ammunition, it meant insufficient performance when firing regular AP shells and - because of difficulties in hitting small mobile targets - its low effective range of about 500 m even with HEAT. The gun also had a quite violent recoil, especially with AP shells. The Germans provided 43 Pak97/38

▲ *The German Pak 97/38 75mm anti-tank gun*

▲ The 50 mm Pak 38, designated by the Hungarians as 38 M. was the first capable anti-tank gun served in the Hungarian Army from the summer of 1942. (War Correspondent Company)

▼ Hungarian Hussars posing around a destroyed 97/38 M. anti-tank gun, the recoil mechanism damaged during the bridge-head battles at the River Don in the summer of 1942. (Deák)   At right: The 75 mm Pak97/38 was a typical stopgap anti-tank gun developed to address the tank panic of the Axis troops due to the Soviet medium and heavy tanks. Hungarians also got the anti-tank guns on the Eastern Front. (War Correspondent Company)

▲ The demonstration of man handling of the 38 M. anti-tank gun presented at Hajmáskér Central Artillery Camp in 1943. The gun had a spare wheel attached to the trail to make it easy to move on the field. (Author's collection)

anti-tank guns to the 2nd Hungarian Army, to improve its anti-tank capability while fighting on the Eastern Front in 1942-1943. The light divisions' anti-tank companies and the 1st Armoured Field Division got the guns. The Germans constantly supplied the Hungarians with the Pak 97/38 anti-tank guns, in December 1942 another four gun were handed over. The transfer of a significant number, 250 guns was planned for 19 January 1943, but the Soviet offensive of 13 January cancelled it.

Technical characteristics

Country of origin	French/German
Specification	Pak 97/38 75mm anti-tank gun
Manufacturer	French Government arsenals
Calibre	75mm L/36
Weight	1190 kg
Projectile weight	6,8 kg
Muzzle velocity	570 m/s
Range	1,5 km with AP shell
Rate of fire	10-14 rounds/minute
Armour penetration	97mm at 100/53mm at 1500 meters
Gun shield	yes
Carriage	split trail
Towing	motorised, 38 M. Botond truck
Crew	6

40 M. 40 M.m anti-tank gun

The 40 M. anti-tank gun was the Hungarian version of the German Pak 36 gun, produced in Hungary, firing the Hungarian designed 40 M.m armoured piercing shell. The 40 M.m Bofors autocannon, the main gun of the 40 M. Turán tank and the 40 M. anti-tank gun fired the same ammunition. The anti-tank gun was horse-drawn or towed by light trucks. Despite its lengthened barrel and increased muzzle velocity and a special armour-piercing grenade it was effective against modern tanks only up to 250 metres. Since there was no prospect of introducing a more modern anti-tank gun until 1944, production of the 40 M. anti-tank cannon, had begun in 1940, continued until the end of the war to provide the Army with a larger number of anti-tank gun. From 1941 until 1944 616 (according to other sources 822) anti-tank guns were manufactured. Until the end of the war the 40 M.m guns served as the main anti-tank weapons of the infantry battalions.

Technical characteristics

Country of origin	Hungary
Specification	40 M. 40 M.m anti-tank gun
Manufacturer	MÁVAG
Calibre	40 M.m L/47
Weight	495kg
Projectile weight	AP 2,25 kg
Rate of fire	20-25 rounds/minute
Muzzle velocity	824 m/s
Range	max 5900 meters
Armour penetration	46mm at 100/30mm at 1000 meters
Gun shield	yes
Carriage	split trail
Towing	horse-drawn or motorised
Crew	6

▲ The German 40 M. Pak 40 75mm anti-tank gun

▲ Hungarian heavy 75 mm 40 M. anti-tank gun in position at a Hungarian village to cover the retreating troops in September 1944. (Magyar Futár)

◄ The 75 mm Pak 40, designated by the Hungarians as 40 M. reached the troops in larger quantity from the summer-autumn of 1944, capable to knock out most of the Soviet tanks. (Magyar Futár)

▲ Hungarian made 40 mm 40 M. anti-tank gun covering the vehicle column of the 2nd Reconnaissance Battalion in April 1944 at Galicia, during the offensive at Nadworna. (ECPA)

40 M. Pak 40 75mm anti-tank gun

The gun was developed in 1939–1941 and entered service in 1942. With 23,303 examples produced, the Pak 40 formed the backbone of German anti-tank guns for the later part of World War II, mostly in towed form, but also on a number of self-propelled artillery such as the Marder series of Panzerjäger. Contracts were placed with Krupp and Rheinmetall to develop what was essentially a 75mm version of the Pak 38. As a result, the Pak 40 used steel throughout its construction and was proportionally heavier than the 50m model. To simplify production, the Pak 38's curved gun shield was replaced by one using three flat plates. The 40 M. anti-tank gun was among the best anti-tank guns of WW2, the 2nd Hungarian Army received six guns in 1942 at River Don, the later larger quantity was handed over to the Hungarians. In 1944 the MÁVAG Factory produced 76 40 M. anti-tank guns under license for the Army. The 40 M. Pak 40 anti-tank guns are towed by 38 M. Botond trucks. At the end of the war the guns were allocated to the heavy anti-tank companies of the divisions and regiments.

Technical characteristics

Country of origin	German
Specification	40 M. 75mm anti-tank gun
Manufacturer	Krupp, Rheinmetall, MÁVAG
Calibre	75mm L/46
Weight	1425 kg
Projectile weight	3,18-6,8 kg
Muzzle velocity	450-990 m/s
Range	1800 max 7600 meters
Armour penetration	143mm at 100/ 77mm at 1500 meters
Gun shield	yes
Carriage	split trail
Towing	motorised, 38 M. Botond truck
Crew	6

Raketenwerfer 43 "Püppchen"

The Raketenwerfer 43 was developed by Erich von Holt at WASAG . It was intended as a replacement for the outdated 2.8 cm heavy Panzerbüchse 41. The rocket launcher looked like a conventional gun but fired rocket ammunition. The carriage with the small protective shield and a spar could be moved on two wheels with solid rubber tires. To reduce the silhouette, the wheels could be removed; the carriage then rested on small sleds. The height was then reduced from 89 cm to 49 cm. The carriage could also be mounted on larger sleds to be able to move it over snow. It was too heavy to be carried by the crew, it could be transported by pack animals in

▲ The Raketenwerfer 43 served with the frontier guard and mountain troops from 1944. (Author's collection)
At right: The Hungarians also got the 88 mm 44 M. heavy anti-tank guns, used in the Carpathian Mountains and later withdraw to Budapest. (MTI)

seven loads or towed by horses or vehicles. The ammunition of the Raketenpanzerbüchse 54 (Panzerschreck) was derived from the previously existing ammunition of the Raketenwerfer 43. The Raketenwerfer 43 had a slightly greater range, the Raketenpanzerbüchse 54 was significantly lighter, easier to transport and to produce with fewer resources. In 1944, Hungarian troops got unknown quantity "Püppchen", according to photo evidence served at the frontier guard/fortress battalions which guarded the mountainous border of Hungary at the Carpathian Mountains.

Technical characteristics

Country of origin	Germany
Specification	Raketenwerfer 43
Manufacturer	WASAG
Calibre	88mm
Length	297 cm
Weight	143 kg
Projectile weight	2,6 kg
Muzzle velocity	110 m/s
Range	500 meters
Armour penetration	160mm
Towing	pack, motorised
Crew	

Pak 43 88mm heavy anti-tank gun

The Pak 43 was the most powerful anti-tank gun of the Wehrmacht. The improved 8.8 cm gun was fitted with a semi-automatic vertical breech mechanism that greatly reduced recoil. It could also be fired electrically while on its wheels. It had a very flat trajectory out to 910 m, making it easier for the gunner to hit targets at longer ranges as fewer corrections in elevation were needed. The gun had exceptional penetration and could defeat the frontal armour of any Allied tank to see service during the war at long range, even the Soviet IS-2 tanks and IS chassis-based tank destroyers. The gun's maximum firing range exceeded 15 km. The main version of the Pak 43 was based on a highly effective cruciform mount, which offered a full 360 degree traverse and a much lower profile than the ubiquitous anti-aircraft 8.8 cm Flak 37. The Pak 43 proved heavy and awkward to handle in the mud and snow of the Eastern Front. The Germans supplied Pak 43 to the Hungarian Army in mid-1944. By November 1944 31 heavy Pak 43 was regrouped from the 1st Hungarian Army to strengthen the defence of Budapest.

Technical characteristics

Country of origin	German
Specification	Pak 43 88mm heavy anti-tank gun
Manufacturer	Krupp
Calibre	88mm L/71
Weight	3650 kg
Projectile weight	7,3 kg
Muzzle velocity	1030mm
Range	150 meters
Rate of fire	6-10 rounds/minute
Armour penetration	238 M.m at 100/153mm at 2000 meter
Gun shield	yes
Carriage	cruciform platform
Towing	motorised
Crew	6+

▲ The 36 M. anti-tank guns soon were modified with pneumatic rubber tires, to make them easy to tow and handle in combat situation. (Mujzer)

► The anti-tank guns were painted in three colour camouflage, the spoked wheeled version remained service up to the early-40s. (Széplaky)

▼ The limber of the 36 M. anti-tank gun with pneumatic rubber tires was also modified. Two crew were seated on the limber, another two stood on the back of the limber. (Author's collection)

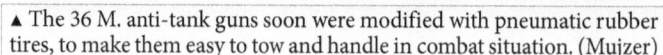

▲ Yugoslavian 37 mm KPÚV vz. 37 Skoda anti-tank gun captured by the Hungarians in April of 1941. The split trailer was folded back for transportation. (Tüzkereszt.com)

▶ The Hungarian 40 M. anti-tank gun was almost identical with the German Pak 36, except the calibre, produced in Hungary. It remained the main anti-tank gun of the battalions until the end of the war. (Service manual)

▼ Pak 40 anti-tank gun towed by the 38 M. Botond truck, belonged to the Heavy Anti-tank Company of the 1st Hussar Division, late 1944 in Hungary. (Illésfalvi)

ARTILLERY

Artillery are ranged weapons that launch munitions far beyond the range and power of infantry firearms. The Hungarian artillery inherited it tactics, weapons and procedures from the Austro-Hungarian artillery of WW1. It consisted of mountain, field, heavy, and anti-aircraft artillery transported by pack animals, horse-drawn, and motor vehicles.

FIELD ARTILLERY
Field artillery is a category of mobile artillery used to support armies in the field. These weapons are specialized for mobility, tactical proficiency, short range, long range, and extremely long-range target engagement. Majority of the field artillery pieces also came from the WW1 area.

15 M. 15/31 M. and 15/35 M. 75mm mountain/cavalry gun
Originally it was a mountain artillery piece but were used by the Hungarians mostly as towed field artillery gun. The Skoda 75mm Gebirgskanone M. 15 was a mountain gun used by Austria-Hungary in WW1. Its development was quite prolonged as the Austrians couldn't decide on the specifications that they wanted. Initially they wanted a gun that could be broken-down into no more than 5 pack-animal loads to replace the various 7 cm mountain guns in service, but prolonged trials proved that the 75mm M. 12 prototype to be the best gun. The guns were delivered beginning in April 1915 instead of the planned date of April 1914. For transport, the gun could be dismantled into 6 parts, generally carried in 4 loads. In addition, there was a gun shield fitted on many such guns. The modified WW1 Skoda Mountain gun served in the Hungarian Artillery. The 15/31 M. gun was towed in one piece by four horse-drawn limbers belonged to the frontier guard battalions' batteries. The 15/35 M. was the cavalry version with larger wheels to serve at Hussar Batteries drawn by six horses, subordinated to the Hussar Regiments. The original 15 M. mountain version served with the mountain and frontier guard battalions designated for mountainous terrain. It was transported by pack animals in eight loads. 70 mountain guns were in service in 1938. Due to the new production and purchase surplus Italian WW1 war booty stocks, 217 15, 15/31 and 15/35 M. guns were in service in 1941. On 24 January 1941, the Italian military attaché addressed a request to the Hungarian MoD to produce such 75/13 model mountain guns for the Italy, because they were in great need of them. Due to lack of industrial capacity this was not done.

Technical characteristics

Country of origin	Austro-Hungary	Austro-Hungary	Hungary
Specification	15 M. mountain gun	15/31 M. cavalry gun	15/35 M. towed mountain gun
Manufacturer	Skoda/MÁVAG	Skoda/MÁVAG	Skoda/MÁVAG
Calibre	75,5mm L/15	75,5mm L/15	75,5mm L/15
Weight	620 kg	770 kg	670 kg
Projectile weight	6,5 kg	6,5 kg	6,5 kg
Muzzle velocity	349 m/s	349 m/s	349 m/s
Range	7600 meters	7600 meters	7600 meters
Rate of fire	5-10 rounds/minute	5-10 rounds/minute	5-10 rounds/minute
Gun shield	yes	yes	yes
Carriage	box trail	box trail	box trail
Towing	pack animals, in six loads	horse-drawn, 6 horses	horse-drawn, 6 horses
Crew	16	6	6

05/08 M. and 18 M. and 22 M. 80mm light field guns
The 80mm Feldkanone 5 M. was a field gun used by Austria-Hungary during WW1. It was a conventional design, with its most notable feature being its obsolescent bronze barrel, necessary because Austria-Hungary still had trouble making steel of the proper quality. These were pre-WW1, outdated designs, due to its weak

▲ *15 M. and 15/31 M. mountain gun.*

▲ The Hungarian Army originated the 75 mm 15 M. mountain guns from the Austro-Hungarian Army, it was widely used between the wars as field artillery pieces. As Hungary regained it mountainous regions, mountain troops were organised with 15 M. guns. (Fortepan/Hanser)

◄ The 35 M. mountain gun was modified for horsed artillery with large wheels, organised into Hussar batteries belonged to the Hussar Regiments. (Mujzer)

▲ The 15/31 M. mountain gun was modified for hors-drawn transportation and one battery served with each frontier guard battalions. (Mujzer)

constructions was not modernized after the war. The Hungarians used the 05/08 M., 18 M. and 22 M. versions of the gun. The 18 M. designed by Böhler, firing a standard shell chambered in 76.5 x 233mm. The 18 M. had better accuracy with the inclusion of a longer barrel, allowing for increased range. In 1922 some 18 M. field artillery pieces were modified to 18/22 M. filed gun. The cannon became lighter and was more suitable for Hussar units too. Some monitors of the Hungarian River Forces were equipped with 22 M. gun armed turrets. The Hungarian armoured trains No. 102 and No. 104 also used the 22 M. guns in their turrets throughout the war. Even the 75mm 41 M. tank gun of the Hungarian 41 M. Turán heavy tank was converted from the 18 M. field gun by the Swedish Bofors. The 41 M. was the first Hungarian tank gun which had a vertical semi-automatic sliding block. The Hungarians had 183 light field guns in service in 1928. Due to the lack suitable artillery pieces it served until 1942 at the light and horsed artillery battalions. By 1942, according to the decision of the Army, the gun was doomed to extinction due to its out-dated characteristics. However, in 1942 the deployed infantry regiments of the 2nd Army on The Eastern Front was reinforced with one-one infantry gun batteries to provide infantry gun support. At the end of the war the 80mm guns were recalled and took part of the fighting in Hungary.

Technical characteristics

Country of origin	Austro-Hungary	Austro-Hungary	Hungary
Specification	05/08 M. field gun	18 M. field gun	22 M. field gun
Manufacturer	Skoda	Bhöler	MÁVAG
Calibre	76,5mm L/30	76,5mm L/33	7,65mm L/30
Weight	1020 kg	1478 kg	
Projectile weight	7 kg	9,9 kg	
Muzzle velocity	500 m/s	500 m/s	
Range	7000 meters	10500 meters	
Rate of fire	10 rounds/minute	10-15 rounds/minute	10 rounds/minute
Armour penetration	75mm at 100 meters with 34/35 M. AP	75mm at 100meters with 34/35 M. AP	75mm at 100m with 34/35 M. AP
Gun shield	yes	yes	yes
Carriage	box trail	box trail	box trail
Towing	horse-drawn, 6 horses	horse-drawn, 6 horses	horse-drawn, 6 horses
Crew	6	6	6

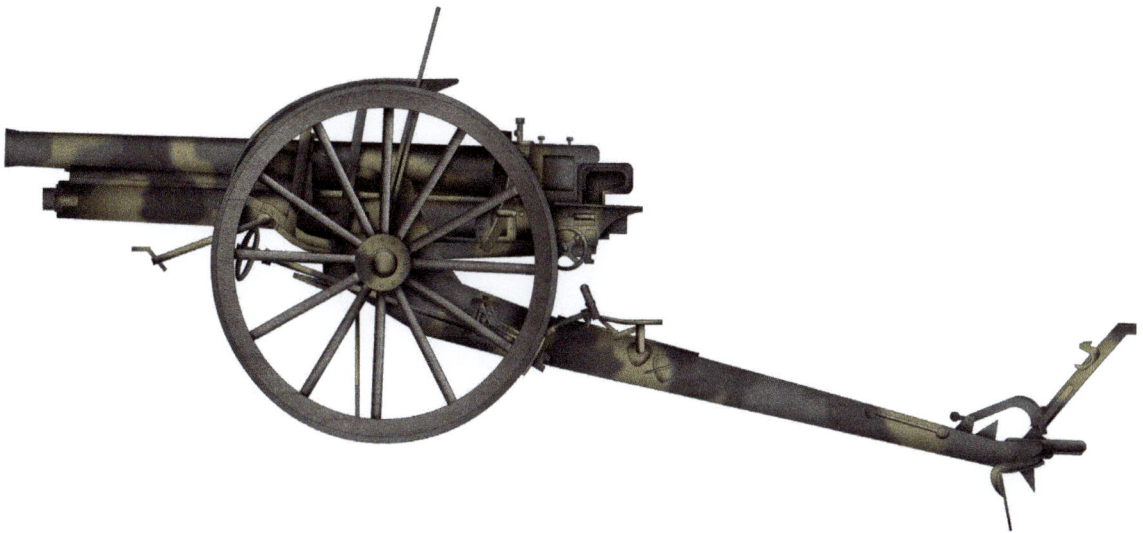

▲ *05/08 M. and 18 M. and 22 M. 80mm light field guns*

14 M. 100mm light field howitzer

The 100mm M. 14 Feldhaubitze was the light howitzer used by Austria-Hungary during WW1. It was a conventional design, the first versions used an obsolescent wrought bronze barrel liner and a cast bronze jacket. Later versions used a standard steel barrel. It was the backbone of the Hungarian field artillery between the wars. It was inherited from the K. und K. Armee, designed by Skoda, considered ballistically and structurally a default design wiht short range, ineffective shell and heavy weight. In 1928 128 pieces of 14 M. light howitzer was in service, another 100 was manufactured in the early 30s. It was kept in service until the end of the war at the field artillery battalions. In early 1942 the Germans handed over 39 ex-Polish 14/19 M. field howitzers, to strengthen the field artillery of 2nd Hungarian Army.

Technical characteristics

Country of origin	Austro-Hungarian	Hungary
Specification	14 M. field howitzer	14/a M. field howitzer
Manufacturer	Skoda, MÁVAG	MÁVAG
Calibre	100 mm L/18	100 mm L/18
Weight	1420 kg	1420 kg
Projectile weight	13,75 kg	11,5 -16 kg
Muzzle velocity	390 m/s	422 m/s
Rate of fire	5 rounds/minute	5 rounds/minute
Range	8870 meters	8870 meters
Gun shield	yes	yes
Carriage	box trail	box trail
Towing	horse-drawn, 6 horses	motorised, by Pavesi tractor
Crew	6	6

▲ *14 M. 100mm light field howitzer*

▲ Gun maintenance of the 80 mm 18 M. Bhöler light guns, the camouflage paint was applied on the back side of the shield. (Fortepan)

◄ A few 80 mm 14 M. anti-aircraft gun was in Hungarian service, the guns served at the River Forces in 20s-30s. (Fortepan/Horváth)

▼ Crew training with horse-drawn 80 mm 05/08 M. light gun. (MTI)

◄▲ Left: The Hungarians experimented the mechanisation of the horse-drawn artillery. The 14 M. got rubber rimmed tires and new limber towed by Pavesi artillery tractor designated as 14/a M. howitzer. (Author's collection) Above: The 14 M. field howitzers although totally outdated actively participated in the WW2, on the Eastern Front. (Author's collection)

◄ Artillery training with 100 mm 14 M. howitzers in the 20s, the field howitzers were the backbone of the Hungarian artillery between the wars. (Mujzer)

▼ The 14 M. field howitzer was towed by six horses, the gun crew consisted of five men transported on the gun and three men looked after the horses, during the occupation of Transylvania in September 1940. (Fortepan/Horváth)

31 M. 105mm motorised gun

The 10.5 cm cannon Model 1927 was a heavy field gun used by the Netherlands and Hungary during World War II. The gun was designed for motor traction with solid rubber tread wheels were made of cast iron. The field gun was similar in design to the 1931 M. 150 mm howitzer, with differences in the longer firing pin, the stronger balancer, the extended firing pin and the smaller pre-shot impact measured in the barrel tail circumference. Its detachable barrel facilitated barrel replacement. The spades were removed and placed onto the trail legs for transport. Hungary purchased the license of the 105mm Swedish Bofors long-range gun towed by motor vehicles in the early 30s. The guns were manufactured at MÁVAG Ordnance Factory; just about 12 guns were produced at Diósgyőr. The gun was towed by Pavesi or Breada artillery tractors. The batteries were organised into a long-range field gun battalion and subordinated directly to the Army High Command, just like the other heavy artillery units. It was the most capable artillery piece of the Army. The number of batteries fired with these guns was few, and they were lost in the winter fighting of 1943.

Technical characteristics

Country of origin	Sweden/Hungary
Specification	31 M. motorised gun
Manufacturer	Bofors/MÁVAG
Calibre	105 mm L/50
Weight	5995 kg
Projectile weight	17,5 kg
Muzzle velocity	825 m/s
Rate of fire	6 rounds/minute
Range	19500 meters
Gun shield	yes
Carriage	split trail
Towing	motorised, in one load by Pavesi tractor
Crew	9

▲ Barrel section 31 M. howitzer, the best artillery piece of the Hungarians in parade in Transylvania, September 1940. (War Correspondent Company)

37 M. 105mm light field howitzer

The 105mm leFH 18 (German: *leichte Feldhaubitze* «light field howitzer») is a German light howitzer used in World War II and the standard artillery piece of the Wehrmacht, adopted for service in 1935 and used by all divisions and artillery battalions. The leFH 18 had a completely new three-point split trail gun carriage provided more stability and increased the traverse. The sighting mechanism made it easier to fire at moving targets. The new gun carriage resulted in a major weight increase to over two tons. The heavier recoil of the higher muzzle velocity of 470 m/s was counteracted by a new pneumatic recuperator above the barrel. A barrel brake containing a water jacket and a fluid equalizer in the upper carriage also checked the recoil. The gun shield was a reinforced, tapered shield with flattened sides that could be folded down. The German sold 40 horses drawn and 44 motorized leFH18 field howitzers to the Hungarians in the late 30s. It was named as 37 M. light howitzer, called by the Hungarians unofficially as "Göring howitzer". The horsed drawn version towed by six horses, the motorized towed by the 37M Hansa Lloyd half-tracked artillery tractor. In case of emergency was used as an anti-tank gun with an armoured piercing shell.

Technical characteristics

Country of origin	Germany
Specification	37 M. light field howitzer
Manufacturer	Reihnmetall-Krupp
Calibre	104,9mm
Weight	horse-drawn 1850 kg, motorised 1900 kg
Projectile weight	14-17,8 kg
Muzzle velocity	471 m/s
Rate of fire	6-8 rounds/minute
Range	10760 meters
Gun shield	yes
Carriage	split trail
Towing	horse-drawn or motorised, Hansa Lloyd half-tracked artillery tractor
Crew	6

▲ Howitzer battery equipped with 37 M. light howitzers in firing position in summer of 1940, preparing for the operation against Romania. The ready to use ammunition positioned next to the howitzer. (Fortepan). Small photo: Platoon commander, ensign holding the shell of the howitzer. The 37 M. howitzers fired 14-17 kilogram shells, the ammunition was cased separate-loading, split into shell and propellant. (Mujzer)

▲ The best artillery piece of the Hungarians was the 105 mm 31 M. Bofors long-range gun, organised into batteries. (Mujzer)

◄ Firing 105mm 37 M. light howitzer during an exercise. The gun crew wearing the light weighted summer uniform.(Mujzer)

▼ The 105mm 37 M. howitzer was quiet heavy, to pull into firing position required 14 gunner, which made the position changings difficult. (Fortepan/Horváth).

below at left: The first modern field artillery piece of the Hungarian Army was the 105mm 37 M. howitzer. The Germans delivered horse-drawn and motorised versions of the howitzer. (Fortepan/Horváth)

Below at right: The hors-drawn version of the 37 M. howitzers were towed by six horses, five men seated on the gun limber, three men riding on the horses. (Fortepan/Horváth)

◄▲ Left: the motorised version of the 105mm 37 M. light howitzers towed by the 37 M. Hansa Lloyd half-tracked (Fortepan/Horváth).

Above: This 37 M. light howitzer belonged to the artillery of the 1st Armoured Field Division took part in the operations and got a direct hit in summer of 1942 at the River Don. (Author's collection)

◄ Motorised howitzer battery equipped with 37 M. howitzers and half-tracked artillery tractors take part in a driving exercise in the late 30s. The Germans delivered the Hansa Lloyd chassis, the body was built in Hungary. (Fortepan/Horváth)

▼ The motorised light howitzers belonged to the motorised and cavalry brigades' light artillery battalions. On the back of 37 M. Hansa Lloyd artillery tractor, the white triangle is the unit sign of an artillery battalion. (Author's collection)

▲ The motorised light howitzer battalions were equipped with 37 M. Hansa Lloyd half-tracked artillery tractors, the ammunition echelon had Ford-Marmon and Botond trucks. (Mujzer)

◄ The 150mm 14 M. medium howitzers were also inherited from the Austro-Hungarian artillery, the heaviest artillery piece to fit into the restriction of the peace treaty. (Author's collection)

▼ The 14 M. medium howitzers were transported in two loads, the barrel and the carriage towed by six-six horses. (Fortepan/Horváth)

Below at left: Hungarian artillery pieces on display, on the left is the carriage system of the 31 M. motorised howitzer, on the right is the 14/39 M. medium howitzer with newly designed muzzle brake. (Mujzer). At right: The Hungarian 40 M. light howitzers also fired the outdated cased separate-loading ammunition, which was identical to the ammunition fired by the German origin light howitzer. (Author's collection)

40 M. 105mm light field howitzer

The Hungarians wanted more leFH18 howitzers, but the Germans declined to sell, at Diósgyőr the MÁVAG Ordnance factory developed a traditional light howitzer horsed and motorized version. The 1940 M. was equipped with a 105mm lightweight barrel muzzle brake, right-handed flat bolt, repeating firing mechanism and safety device against premature and accidental firing, a gun shield and a locker-mounted firing pin. The howitzer could fire the ammunition of the 105mm German-made leFH 18 howitzers (in Hungarian Ordnance 37 M. howitzer) without any modification. To achieve a projectile velocity of about 510 m/s, it was necessary to systemise a spare charge. Its wheels were solid rubber tyre wheels. It had both a tandem (6 horses) and a mechanised version. No reliable data are available on the production quantities of the 105mm 40 M. light field howitzer. After long trials, the production started in 1942 and by the end of 1944 at least 141 pieces of 40 M. light howitzer was produced. Interestingly the barrel of the howitzer was used for the 40/43 M. Zrínyi assault howitzer too. Later a motorised version was designed as 42 M. light howitzer

Technical characteristics

Country of origin	Hungary	Hungary
Specification	40 M. light field howitzer	42 M. light field howitzer
Manufacturer	MÁVAG	MÁVAG
Calibre	104,9mm L/14	104,9mm L/14
Weight	1550 kg	1600 kg
Projectile weight	14,81 kg	14,81 kg
Muzzle velocity	442 m/s	442 m/s
Rate of fire	7 rounds/minute	7 rounds/minute
Range	10760 meters	11250 meters
Gun shield	yes	yes
Carriage	box trail	split trail
Towing	horse-drawn, one loads, 6 horses	motorised, one loads
Crew	6	6

▲ Left: The Hungarian 40 M. light howitzer, although was designed in early 40s, but was an old design with box trail carriage. (Sárhidai). At right: The artillery battalions got their 40 M. light howitzer in 1943-1944, took part of the operations in 1944-1945. (Author's collection)

14 M., 14/39 M. 150mm medium howitzer

The 15 cm schwere Feldhaubitze M 14 was a heavy howitzer which served with Austria-Hungary during WW1. The Škoda 15 cm M 14 was developed and built at the Škoda Works in Pilsen. Like other guns of the time, it had two crew seats mounted on the Gun shield. It broke down into two loads for transport. The M 14 was modified to improve elevation and range as well as to strengthen the carriage as the M 14/16. It was a good heavy field howitzer with a steel barrel and quick-firing thanks to its modern hydro-spring recoil recuperation system, this weapon was manufactured in more than 1000 items. It was largely distributed to the units of the heavy field artillery. It was normally transported in two separate loads but could also be hauled in a single load with an ammunition trailer. A lightened mountain version was studied in 1918. The M 14 and M 14/16 was kept in service by Hungary as 14 M. medium howitzer. Hungarian weapons were upgraded in 1935 by MAVAG and designated as 14/35 M. Later in 1939 another batch of guns were updated and designated as14/39 M. Due to the modernization in 1935 and 1939, got a longer barrel and a muzzle brake to balance it, which improved its range to 10700 meters. These were the main medium artillery weapons of the brigade and divisional artillery, transported in two loads, barrel and carriage towed by six horses each. 49 was in service in 1928. From 1938 until 1944, 127 14/39 M. medium field howitzers were manufactured.

Technical characteristics

Country of origin	Austro-Hungarian	Hungary	Hungary
Specification	14 M. medium howitzer	14/35 M. medium howitzer	14/39 M. medium howitzer
Manufacturer	Skoda/MÁVAG	Skoda/MÁVAG	Skoda/MÁVAG
Calibre	149,1mm L/14	149mm L/14	149mm L/14
Weight	2765 kg	2965 kg	2965 kg
Projectile weight	42 kg	42-47 kg	42-47 kg
Muzzle velocity	350 m/s	277-380 m/s	345 m/s
Rate of fire	6 rounds/minute	6 rounds/minute	6 rounds/minute
Range	8000 meters	10700 meters	10700 metres
Gun shield	yes	yes	yes
Carriage	box trai	box trail	box trail
Towing	horse-drawn, two loads, 6 horses each	horse-drawn, two loads, 6 horses each	horse-drawn, two loads, six horses each
Crew	8	8	8

▲ *14/39 M. 150mm medium howitzer*

▲ The 14/39 M. medium howitzers fought until the end of the WW2, this picture was taken in April 1944 in Galicia, and this howitzer belonged to the artillery of the 24th Infantry Division. (ECPA).

31 M. 150mm motorised medium howitzer

The Hungarians purchased the Swedish Bofors Factory medium howitzer in the early 30s, also produced by the MÁVAG Ordnance Factory. The 1931 M. 150 mm medium motorised field howitzer had a chrome-nickel steel, single-walled barrel. Locking mechanism with screw lock "de Bange" seal. It featured self-actuated reverse roll control, fluid brake, air release, independent directional control with independent guideline, fully rearward mounted trunnions. It was fitted with coil thrusters for traction and disc thrusters for firing. The howitzer was towed by 29 M. Pavesi artillery tractors in two sections, barrel, and carriage, in case of changing position the howitzer could be transported in one unit. The 31 M. medium howitzers belonged to the Corps level artillery. Altogether 30 medium howitzers were manufactured during the war.

Technical characteristics

Country of origin	Sweden/Hungary
Specification	31 M. motorised medium howitzer
Manufacturer	Bofors/MÁVAG
Calibre	149,1mm L/24
Weight	5595 kg
Projectile weight	42/47 kg
Muzzle velocity	530-583 m/s
Rate of fire	
Range	14600 meters
Gun shield	yes
Carriage	split trail
Towing	motorised, one or two loads, Pavesi or Breda tractors
Crew	8

◄▲ The 150mm 31 M. medium howitzer ready for fire, the howitzer also fired cased separate-loading ammunition. (Mujzer)

Above: Artillery man dressed in woollen slew leather jerkin stand on the carriage behind the lock of the 31 M. medium howitzer. (Mujzer)

◄ The 210mm 39/40 M. heavy howitzer was the most modern heavy artillery piece of the Hungarian artillery at Hajmáskér Central Artillery School. (Mujzer)

▼ The 31 M. medium howitzer battalions belonged to the Corps' artillery and were deployed to the Eastern Front in summer of 1942.

39 M., 40 M. 210mm towed heavy howitzer

According to the expansion of the Hungarian heavy artillery seven heavy artillery battalions (3 batteries/2 howitzers) plus 6 spare one, altogether 48 heavy howitzers should serve by December 1940 in the heavy artillery battalions. The Hungarians selected the Italian howitzer for home production, although it was not yet mass produced that time. However, due to the time pressure 8 heavy howitzers were ordered from Italy in 1938. The first, experimental howitzer was sent by the end of the year. Due to the tests some engineering modification had to be performed. Also, the Italian production was delayed, the first two howitzers were promised in 1939, the remaining six only in 1940. They were found to be unsuitable for long-range towing due to problems with the tracked mountings. Improvements were made, which resulted in the 40 M. heavy howitzer. The Hungarians manufactured howitzers under license. The heavy howitzers were towed by separate sections of barrel and carriage by 32 M. Breda heavy artillery tractors. Nevertheless, in the autumn of 1941 the first 40 M. Hungarian 210mm howitzer was delivered in Diósgyőr, which proved to be considerably more usable than the original version.

Technical characteristics

Country of origin	Italy	Hungary
Specification	39 M. heavy howitzer	40 M. heavy howitzer
Manufacturer	Ansaldo/MÁVAG	MÁVAG
Calibre	210mm L/23,8	210mm L/23,8
Weight	15885 kg	15885 kg
Projectile weight	101-117,5 kg	101-117,5bkg
Muzzle velocity	528-553 m/s	528-553m/s
Range	15400 meters	15400 meters
Rate of fire	3-4 rounds/minute	3-4 rounds/minute
Gun shield	no	no
Carriage	split trail	split trail
Towing	motorised, in two loads	motorised, in two loads
Crew	12	12

▲ *39 M., 40 M. 210mm towed heavy howitzer*

▲ The 39/40 M. heavy howitzers were towed by 32 M. Breda heavy artillery tractors in two loads, during the occupation of Transylvania in September 1940. (Fortepan)

▼ The 39/41 M. heavy howitzers fought on the Eastern Front, at River Don. The crew serving the heavily camouflaged howitzers in the summer of 1942. (War Correspondent Company)

▲ Gun layer of the 39/41 M. heavy howitzer during the bridge head battles at River Don in summer of 1942. (War Correspondent Company)

◄ Elevated barrel of the 210mm 39/40 M. heavy howitzer of the Hungarian heavy artillery. The howitzers were also painted in three colours camouflage. (Author's collection)

11/16 M. 305mm siege howitzer

Škoda Works was tasked to develop a weapon capable of penetrating the concrete fortresses being built in Belgium and Italy. Development work continued until 1909, when the first prototype was finished and, in 1910, fired secretly in Hungary. The weapon was able to penetrate 2 m of reinforced concrete with its special armour-piercing shell, which weighed 384 kg. The weapon was transported in three sections by a 100-horsepower 15-ton Austro-Daimler M 12 artillery tractor. It broke down into barrel, carriage and firing platform loads, each of which had its own trailer. It could be assembled and readied to fire in around 50 minutes. The mortar could fire two types of shell, a heavy armour-piercing shell with a delayed action fuse and a lighter 287 kg shell fitted with an impact fuse. The light shell could create a crater 8 meters wide and 8 meters deep, as well as killing exposed infantry up to 400 m away. After firing, it automatically returned to the horizontal loading position. After WW1 five Skoda siege howitzer remained in Hungarian hands, dismantled and hidden. Later put back into service. The siege howitzers were transported by 32M Breda heavy artillery tractors. The siege howitzers deployed in the Yugoslav Campaign in 1941 and on the Eastern Front in 1942. Ammunition for the 5 existing 305mm siege mortars was also hidden from the Entente's inspection committees. In the period from about 1930 to 1937, these ammunitions were used for training and gunnery. The shells often on impact slipped, broke and did not explode, even on flat ground. Due to the sudden demand for ammunition Italian supply helped. Estimated quantity purchased: 4500-5000 shells. The ammunition was of First World War design. Nevertheless, they were reliable.

Technical characteristics

Country of origin	Austro-Hungarian
Specification	11/16 M. siege howitzer
Manufacturer	Skoda
Calibre	305mm L/10
Weight	20830 kg
Projectile weight	300-385 kg
Muzzle velocity	229-371 m/s
Range	11250 meters
Rate of fire	10-12/hours
Gun shield	no
Carriage	2600x4600 platform
Towing	motorised
Crew	15-17

▲ Assembling together the barrel section with the firing platform of the 305mm 16 M. siege mortar during the preparation against Romania in 1940. (Fortepan/Horváth)

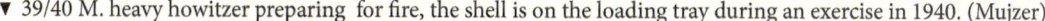
▲ Officers inspecting the 16 M. siege mortar in firing position in summer of 1940. The Hungarian officers wearing the non-issued trench coats. (Author's collection)
▼ 39/40 M. heavy howitzer preparing for fire, the shell is on the loading tray during an exercise in 1940. (Mujzer)

▲ Above: the firing platform of the 305mm 16 M. sige mortar towed by the 32 M. Breda heavy artillery tractor in September 1940, Transylvania. (Fortepan)

Below: the 16 M. siege mortars were also towed by the 32 M. Breda heavy artillery tractors in three separated loads, during the occupation of Transylvania in 1940. (Fortepan)

◀ Barrel of the 16 M. siege mortar. (Author's collection)

ANTI-AIRCRAFT ARTILLERY

The anti-aircraft guns are fired from the ground or shipboard in defence against aerial attack. Anti-aircraft weapons development began as early as 1910, when the airplane first became an effective weapon. In World War II, rapid-firing and automatic antiaircraft guns were introduced, radar was applied to target tracking, and tiny radio-wave proximity fuses exploded the ammunition as it approached the target. Heavier antiaircraft guns, up to 120 mm, were used against high-flying bombers. In late 20es, the Hungarian Army choose the Swedish Bofors anti-aircraft gun, followed by 40 M.m autocannon in mid 30s. The Hungarian anti-aircraft artillery had an advantage to use the Gamma-Juhasz anti-aircraft battery fire control calculator, designed by István Juhász of Hungary. The predictor operated geometrically, using the set points to create a 1:40,000 scaled down predicting triangle, which gave the coordinates of the advance point. At the time, the predictor was extremely advanced as it was able of following a target that was either making a turn or rapidly changing altitude.

05/08 M. 80mm truck mounted anti-aircraft gun

This Austro-Hungarian gun, however, cannot be classified as a simple improvisation, but was an attempt at producing a real anti-aircraft gun, albeit using a normal field gun. The gun itself is the standard Austro-Hungarian Field Gun, the M.5/8, but by placing the gun on a high-angle pedestal mount with 360 ° traverse and firing shrapnel shell, designed by Skoda. The gun was called 8cm Luftfahrzeugabwehr-Kanone M5/8 M.P., M.P. standing for Mittelpivotlafette. It had an elevation between -10° and +80°. It could shoot a 6.6kg shrapnel shell, which was the standard shell against the aircrafts. In 1919, two 05/08 M. anti-aircraft guns remained in Hungary without sights and transportation. The Hungarians ordered 20 anti-aircraft guns from the Gun Factory at Diósgyőr in 1920, the calibre of the guns fitted into the restriction of the peace treaty. However, take position with the gun on heavy pedestal mounting was extremely time consuming, difficult, it worked as fixed weapon. In 1925, based on German examples the 05/08 M. anti-aircraft gun was put on the Rába V. truck. The Rába V. produced by the MÁVAG, was a 3-tonne truck, with solid rubber wheels. It was the best vehicles what the home production was able to manufacture. The truck could carry the gun, the 13 men crew and 50 ready to use ammunition. The 05/08 M. guns were organised into five anti-aircraft gun batteries. A truck mounted anti-aircraft battery consisted of one battery commander car, three sidecar motorbikes, four Rába V. trucks with 05/08 M. anti-aircraft guns, four small truck of the command and protection element of the battery, four ammunition and four other trucks for baggage, food, kitchen and maintenance. To circumvent the restriction of the peace treaty, in late 20s, within the River Forces, which did not belong to the Army that time an anti-aircraft battalion was organised. The gun was not meet the modern requirements, 50-60 shots/year burned out the barrels, the screws of the fire control devices were worn out. The Army focused on the licence production of the Swedish Bofors anti-aircraft gun. Already from the beginning of 30s planned to withdraw from the active service. However, the guns remained in service until 1944 at the home air defence.

Technical characteristics

Country of origin	Austro-Hungary
Specification	5/8 M. anti-aircraft gun
Manufacturer	Skoda
Calibre	80mm L/48
Weight	2470 kg
Projectile weight	6,6 kg
Muzzle velocity	500 m/s
Horizontal range	7000 meters
Altitude range	3800 meters
Rate of fire	15-18 rounds/minutes
Gun shield	no
Carriage	mounted on Rába V. truck
Towing	truck borne
Crew	13

▲ The 80mm 05/08 M. anti-aircraft gun was mounted on a Rába V. truck to provide mobility for the cumbersome weapon in the early 20s. (Author's collection)

▼ To circumvent the restriction of the peace treaty the 05/08 M. anti-aircraft guns grouped under the cover of the River Forces, which that time did not belonged to the Army, the crew had sailor uniform too. (Author's collection)

29 M., 29/38 M. 80mm Bofors anti-aircraft gun

The Hungarians purchased the license rights of the 80mm Bofors anti-aircraft gun from the Bofors Factory, Sweden in 1929. The guns are assigned to the gun batteries of the anti-aircraft battalions. Although the gun had good ballistic characteristics it was difficult and time-consuming to make it ready to fire. The modified 29/38 M. gun got a muzzle brake which reduced the recoil. From 1929 until 1944 the Ordnance Factory manufactured 102 anti-aircraft guns. The Bofors guns were towed by 28 M. Pavesi and later KV-40 artillery tractors. From 1941, it was clear that the 29 M. guns not fitted to frontline duties, the divisions got autocannons, the 29 M. guns mostly serves at Home Defence artillery battalion.

Technical characteristics

Country of origin	Sweden/Hungary	Hungary
Specification	29 M. anti-aircraft gun	29/38/44 M. anti-aircraft gun
Manufacturer	Bofors/MÁVAG	MÁVAG
Calibre	80mm L/48	80mm L48
Weight	3309 kg	3340 kg
Projectile weight	8 kg	8 kg
Muzzle velocity	750 m/s	880-910 m/s
Horizontal range	14900 meters	11500 meters
Altitude range	9300 meters	10800 meters
Rate of fire	15-18 rounds/minutes	15-18 rounds/minutes
Armoure penetration	75mm at 2000-meter 29/35 M. AP	75mm at 2000-meter 29/35 M. AP
Gun shield	no	no
Carriage	cruciform firing platform	cruciform firing platform
Towing	motorised, one loads	motorised, one loads
Crew	9	9

37M German, 39r.M 88mm, and 39 M. 105mm anti-aircraft guns

From autumn of 1944, the Germans handed over modern anti-aircraft guns to the Hungarians because they had no crew for manning them. The Hungarian anti-aircraft units got 86 German 88mm, 78 re-barrelled ex-Soviet 85mm 39.r M. anti-aircraft guns, and 30 39 M. 105mm heavy anti-aircraft guns used by the Home Defence Anti-aircraft artillery until the end of the war. The captured Soviet guns were rechambered for 88mm shells.

Technical characteristics

Country of origin	Germany	Soviet Union	Germany
Specification	37 M. anti-aircraft gun	39r. M 85 anti-aircraft gun	39 M. anti-aircraft gun
Manufacturer			Rehinmetall
Calibre	88mm L56	88mm L/55,2	105mm L/52,8
Weight	5000 kg	4300 kg	10224 kg
Projectile weight	9,5 kg	9,2 kg	15,1 kg
Muzzle velocity	820 m/s	797 m/s	881 m/s
Horizontal range	14860 meters	15500 metres	17300 meters
Altitude range	10600 meters	10500 meters	10500 meters
Rate of fire	15 rounds/minute	10-12 rounds/minute	15 rounds/minute
Armour penetration	84mm at 2000 meters	78mm at 2000 meters	no
Gun shield	no	no	no
Carriage	cruciform firing platform	cruciform firing platform	cruciform firing platform
Towing	motorised	motorised	motorised
Crew	10	7	10

▲ 29 M. Bofors anti-aircraft gun deployed to the River Don, covering a Hungarian higher command post, engaging Soviet aircrafts. (Fortepan/Konok)

▼ The 29 M. Bofors anti-aircraft gun in firing position on cruciform platform, behind the gun the ammunition limber and the water tower of the Hajmáskér Central Artillery Camp are visible. (Fortepan/Alföldy)

▲ The Anti-Aircraft Artillery used Pavesi and Hungarian KV-40 tractors to pull the guns. On this picture a KV-40 artillery tractor towing the 29 M. gun and its limber. (Fortepan)

▼ The Hungarian anti-aircraft artillery had an advantage to use the Gamma-Juhasz anti-aircraft battery fire control calculator, designed by István Juhász of Hungary. It was a successful product sold for foreign countries. (Fortepan/Horváth).

At right: The 29 M. anti-aircraft guns were less mobile due to the complicated gun platform, were able to fire from fixed positions. (Original colour photo)

36 M. 40 M.m Bofors anti-aircraft autocannon

The MÁVAG Factory produced the Swedish Bofors autoautocannon from 1936. It was one of the best Hungarian weapons during the war. The autocannon was primarily used as an anti-aircraft autocannon, but during the first part of the war used as a gap stop anti-tank weapon, later used against land targets too. In 1942 the autocannon got an armoured shield, designated as 36/40 M. Bofors autoautocannon. The Hungarians manufactured 878 Bofors autocannons from 1936 until 1944. About 220 Bofors were produced for the Germans during the war too. The Bofors autocannons were towed by Ford-Marmon or 38 M. Botond trucks. The Italians also interested in the Hungarian made 40 M.m Bofors autocannon. On 7 July 1941, the Italian military attasche, Collonel Emilio Voli asked five Bofors autocannon, 2.000 shells to be send to Nettunia for testing. At the end of the war the anti-aircraft autocannon batteries belonged to the infantry divisions, consisted of six Bofors cannons. As the military situation deteriorated, from autumn of 1944, the Bofors autocannons were deployed for delayed actions, in anti-tank role, took ambush positions and using, covering the withdrawing infantry. The Bofors, as well as the Nimród self-propelled armoured anti-aircraft cannons got the Stielgranate 41 a German shaped charge, fin-stabilized shell, adopted for the 40 M.m calibre to give better anti-tank performance. Now the Bofors could penetrate most armour, although the low velocity of the projectile limited its range. The frontal reloading was another problem.

Technical characteristics

Country of origin	Sweden/Hungary
Specification	36 M. 40 M.m anti-aircraft autocannon
Manufacturer	MÁVAG
Calibre	40 M.m
Weight	2100 kg
Projectile weight	955gr.
Muzzle velocity	850 m/s
Horizontal range	7000 meters
Altitude range	3000 meters
Rate of fire	120 rounds/minute, four rounds in clip
Armour penetration	AP rounds
Gun shield	40 M. yes
Carriage	four wheeled platform
Towing	motorised
Crew	9

▲ 36 M. autocannon in firing position against land targets, on the left a 36 M. 125mm Süss-Goerz the rangefinder is visible. (Fortepan/Korner)

▲ The 29 M. gun was modified, got a muzzle brake which improve its range, named 29/42 M. anti-aircraft gun.

▼ The modified version of the Bofors gun, the 29/38 M. got muzzle brake, with better range and velocity. The gun on the photo had at least eight white stripes on the barrel, two other coloured stripes maybe symbolised land targets. (Author's collection)

▲ The Hungarian also got some captured ex-Soviet 39r. M 85 anti-aircraft gun rechambered for 88mm shells. The photo taken during the siege of Budapest, Red Army soldiers passing an abandoned gun in 1945. (Fortepan/Vörös Hadsereg)

◄ The Hungarian Home Defence anti-aircraft artillery got some 36 M. 88mm German anti-aircraft guns, on the picture some of the crew holding the shells wearing leather pilot helmets. (Author's collection)

▲ 80mm Bofors 29 M. anti-aircraft guns firing for land targets, the velocity of the shell abled the gun to use in anti-tank role, however the difficulty handling and high profile made it unfit for this task. (Fortepan/Horváth)

▼ The 36 M. Bofors cannons provide cover for the troops crossing the River Dniester in July 1941, behind the cannon pontoons are visible. (Author's collection)

▲ The new shield of the 36/42 M. also allowed the high travers of the canon, this one got eight victories. (Magyar Futár)

◄ Original designed as anti-aircraft cannon, the 36 M. Bofors soon become a dual-purpose artillery piece, it was very accurate, quick firing artillery piece against land/soft targets. (Mujzer)

▲ 40 M.m Bofors 36 M. autocannon was the light anti-aircraft artillery peace of the Hungarian Army, the photo taken during the Yugoslavian Campaign in April 1941. (Fortepan/Fehér)

▼ According to the lessons learned from the operation, the Bofors got armoured shield to protect the crew, it was designated as 36/42 M autocannon. (HIM HL)

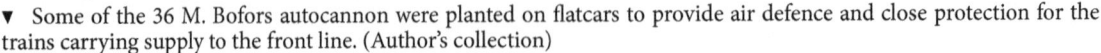

▲ 80mm Bofors 29 M. gun in firing position, the ammunition boxes laid next to the gun, the two wheeled carriage seen on the right. (Fortepan/Horváth)

▼ Some of the 36 M. Bofors autocannon were planted on flatcars to provide air defence and close protection for the trains carrying supply to the front line. (Author's collection)

ROCKET LAUNCHERS

Modern rocket artillery was first employed during World War II, in the form of the German Nebelwerfer family of rocket ordnance designs, and Soviet Katyusha-series, and numerous other systems employed on a smaller scale by the Western allies and Japan. The Hungarians were issued with German multiple rocket launcher systems form 1943, later it had a domestic production too.

40. and 43 M. 150mm Multiple Rocket Launcher

The 150mm Nebelwerfer 41 (15 cm NbW 41) was a German multiple rocket launcher used in the Second World War. It served with units of the *Nebeltruppen*, German Chemical Corps units that had the responsibility for poison gas and smoke weapons that were also used to deliver high-explosives during the war. It was fired from a six-tube launcher mounted on a towed carriage adapted from that used by the 37mm Pak 36 to a range of 6,900 metres, later also mounted on a halftrack. The 2nd Hungarian Army got 27 40 M. Nebelwerfer from the Germans on the front in January 1943, organized into the 102nd Smoke Launcher Artillery Regiment. The Hungarians purchased the license of the 150mm Nebelwerfer, produced by the Weiss Manfred Factory named 43 M. multiply rocket launcher. Four multiply rocket launcher battalion was organized with 18 multiply rocket launchers each directly subordinated to the High Command. Took part in the operations in Galicia and Hungary in 1944-1945.

Technical characteristics

Country of origin	Germany
Specification	40. and 43 M. 150mm Multiple Rocket Launcher
Manufacturer	Weiss Manfréd
Calibre	6x158mm
Weight	770 kg
Projectile weight	6x31-35 kg
Muzzle velocity	342 m/s
Range	6900 meters
Gun shield	no
Carriage	split trail
Towing	motorised, self-propelled
Crew	5

▲ Due to the light weight of the multi rocket launcher systems were towed by Krupp Protze and Botond trucks. (Sárhidai)

44 M. Buzogány (Mace) twin anti-tank rocket launcher

It was an unguided anti-tank rocket designed in Hungary for use against Soviet heavy tanks and infantry during World War II. In 1942, the HTI (Institute of Military Technology) began work to develop a cheap and easy to produce weapon capable of destroying Soviet heavy tanks after Germans was unwilling to share technology related to their work on an experimental wire-guided missile. The first prototype was completed in the spring of 1944 and underwent testing in the military training field of Esztergom. After recommendations from troops who tested the weapon were considered, it was approved for production in the summer of 1944. The weapon consisted of two launch tubes mounted on either a captured Maxim M1910 or Goryunov machine gun or installed on Krupp Protze truck. A large, thin metal shield separated the firing mechanism of the weapon from the launch tubes in order to protect the gunner from the back-blast of the weapon›s initial propulsion charge. The gun used a machine gun sight to aim and had two paddle like triggers on the bar-like hand holds the gunner would hold on to while aiming the weapon. The Weiss Manfréd produced 600-700 rocket launchers, mainly deployed around Budapest, late 1944. Between 3 and 4 January 1945, the 44M Buzogány launchers knocked out nine Soviet T-34 tanks.

Technical characteristics

Country of origin	Hungary
Specification	44M Buzogány (Mace) twin anti-tank rocket launcher
Manufacturer	Weiss Manfréd
Diameter	215mm
Weight	?
Projectile weight	HEAT 4,2 kg
Muzzle velocity	56 m/s
Rate of fire	6 rounds/minutes
Armour penetration	300mm
Range	500-1200 meters
Gun shield	no
Carriage	tripod, two-wheel
Towing	truck mounted or transported
Crew	3-4

▲ Hungarian artillery men training with the 40/43 M. multi rocket launcher system at Hajmáskér, in 1943-1944. The formed multi rocket launcher artillery battalions were directly subordinated to the High Command. (Author's collection)

▲ The 44 M. Mace anti-tank rocket system was an awkward looking, gap stop anti-tank rocket system designed by the Hungarian Military Technical Institute produced by the Weiss Manfréd Factory. (Sárhidai)

▼ The rocket had a 4,2-kilogram warhead which was able to penetrate any kind of armour plate of it time. The 44 M. Mace were deployed around Budapest in late 1944. (Sárhidai)

BIBLIOGRAPHY

Balázs József -Pongó János: *Pisztolyok és revolverek*. Budapest, Zrínyi Kiadó. 1977.

Barczy Zoltán – Sárhidai Gyula: *A Boforstól a Doráig*. Budapest, Petit Military Könyvek, 2008.

Bishop, Chris: *Encyclopedia, Weapons of the World War II*. New York, Metro Books, 2002.

Dombrády Lóránt-Germuska Pál-Kovács Géza Péter-Kovács Vilmos: *A Magyar hadiipar története. A kezdetektől napjainking*. Budapest, Zrínyi Kiadó, 2016.

Csillag Ferenc: *A kézi lőfegyverek és a hadművészet*. Budapest, Zrínyi Kiadó, 1965.

Eötvös Péter- Hatala andrás-Soós Péter: *A Király géppisztoly*. Budapest, Zrínyi Kiadó, 2014.

Ford, Roger: *The world's great machine guns, from 1860 to the present day*. London, Brown Books, 1999.

Gander, Terry J.: *The 40 M.m Bofors gun*. Wellingborough, Patrick Stephens Ltd. 1986.

Hogg, Ian V.-Weeks, John S.: *Military Small Arms of the 20th Century*. Iola, Krause Publication, 2000.

Hogg, Ian: *Twentieth-Century Artillery*. Hoo, Grange Books, 2000.

Kováts Zoltán-Lugosi József-Nagy István-Sárhidai Gyula: *Tábori tüzérség*. Budapes, Zrínyi Kiadó, 1988.

Kováts Zoltán-Nagy István: *Kézi lőfegyverek*. Budapest, Zrínyi Kiadó, 1986.

Lucas, James: *German Army Handbook 1939-1945*. Thrupp, Sutton Publishing Ltd. 1998.

McNab, Chris: *Twentieth-Century Small Arms*. Hoo, Grange Books, 2001.

Szanati József: *A tábori tüzérség az első és a második világháborúban*. Budapest, Zrínyi Kiadó 1984.

Varga József alezredes: *A légvédelmi tüzérség története a kezdetektől a második világháború végéig*. Budapest, MH kiadvány, 1995.

Quarrie, Bruce: *Encyclopedia of the German Army in the 20th Century*. Wellingborough, Patrick Stephens Ltd. 1989.

Luca S.Cristini: *German anti-tank guns (PAK)*. Soldiershop Italy 2024

Luca S.Cristini: *Italian Artillery 1914-1945 – Vol. 2*. Soldiershop Italy 2024

Book of the Author about Hungarian army in WW2

Péter Mujzer: *Hungarian army at the Barbarossa campaign in 1941*. Soldiershop Italy 2024

Péter Mujzer: *Italian tanks trucks and weapons in Hungarian service*. Soldiershop Italy 2024

Péter Mujzer: *Hungarian 39/40 M. Csaba & 40/43 M. Zrínyi*. Soldiershop Italy 2024

TITOLI GIÀ PUBBLICATI - TITLES ALREADY PUBLISHING

WTW-064 EN

www.ingramcontent.com/pod-product-compliance
Lightning Source LLC
LaVergne TN
LVHW072120060526
838201LV00068B/4927